EVERYMAN'S
BIBLE
COMMENTARY

FIRST & SECOND
THESSALONIANS

EVERYMAN'S
BIBLE
COMMENTARY

FIRST & SECOND
THESSALONIANS

Charles C. Ryrie

MOODY PRESS
CHICAGO

Library of Congress Cataloging-in-Publication Data

Ryrie, Charles Caldwell, 1925–
    First and Second Thessalonians / Charles Caldwell Ryrie.
        p. cm. -- (Everyman's Bible commentary)
    Includes bibliographical references.
    ISBN 0-8024-7110-2
    1. Bible. N.T. Thessalonians--Commentaries. I. Title. II. Series.
BS2725.3 .R97 2001
227′.8107--dc21   00-046922

1 3 5 7 9 10 8 6 4 2

Printed in the United States of America

CONTENTS

BACKGROUND OF THE
THESSALONIAN LETTERS

Every once in a while a new book will appear on the market with a title something like this: *How I've Changed My Mind.* The various chapters then detail the ways in which the author's thinking has changed (often about important doctrines) throughout his lifetime. The apostle Paul would never have written such a book. Here's why we can be certain of that.

Although among the earliest of Paul's letters (only Galatians is earlier), 1 and 2 Thessalonians in no way exhibit undeveloped or immature thinking. Paul had been a Christian for seventeen or eighteen years by the time he wrote 1 Thessalonians. Furthermore, he had been a missionary for seven or eight years and had written Galatians, a letter filled with meaty and important doctrines. His theology was fully developed in his mind and tested in his ministry before he wrote these letters to the Thessalonians.

These epistles are like finely cut gems. They reflect the depths of theological thought, especially in the area of future things. They mirror the pattern of teaching that the apostle used with new Gentile converts. From every part shine forth the character and conduct of Paul's missionary heart, and they sparkle with the brilliance of the captivating power of the

Gospel of the grace of Christ. They are a joy to read and a delight to study.

THE BEGINNING OF PAUL'S SECOND MISSIONARY TRIP, ACTS 15:36–17:9

1. *The purpose of the trip, 15:36.* Not to evangelize but to revisit the churches established on the first journey to see how they were faring was the purpose of the second trip.
2. *The sharp disagreement, 15:37–41.* Paul's unwillingness to take John Mark along, because he had deserted the team partway through the first trip, and Barnabas's insistence that they include Mark provoked a sharp disagreement between the two leaders. The outcome saw two teams going out in different directions: Paul and Silas, and Barnabas and Mark.
3. *The addition of Timothy, 16:1–5.* When Paul and Silas came to Lystra, they added Timothy to the team.
4. *The call to go to Europe, 16:6–10.* Having come from the east, the group was forbidden to go west into Asia Minor and north into Bithynia. So they traveled in a northwesterly direction around Asia Minor, arriving eventually at Troas. There they waited for the Lord's leading and received it in the form of a vision of a Greek man (who represented the finest of intelligent, civilized, and cultured humanity of that day) calling them to Greece in Europe.
5. *The ministry in Philippi, 16:11–40.* This included the conversion of Lydia and her associates, the exorcism of a demon-possessed girl, being imprisoned, released by an earthquake, and the conversion of the jailer's household.
6. *The ministry in Thessalonica, 17:1–9.*

THE CITY OF THESSALONICA

ITS HISTORY

In Paul's day, Thessalonica (now Salonika) was an important city. Its history had made it so, for in 315 B.C., Cassander, son of Antipater, reconstructed Therma (named for its hot

springs) into a fine metropolis and gave it the name Thessalonica after his wife, who was the daughter of Philip of Macedon
and half sister of Alexander. Under the Romans, the city was the
capital of the newly formed province and its largest city. It had a
population of about 200,000 (around 300,000 today).

ITS LOCATION

Thessalonica's strategic location also contributed to its
importance. It was one of the greatest, if not the greatest, of the
cities along the entire Egnatian Road, a great military highway
that connected Rome with the east and ran parallel to the sea
line of communication by way of Corinth. Situated at the north-
western corner of the Aegean Sea, its sheltered harbor was made
into a naval station and equipped with docks by the Romans. Its
location midway between the Adriatic and the Hellespont makes
it even today a natural outlet for traffic from all points.

This commercial activity had two important results. First, it
made Thessalonica a wealthy city. Well-to-do Romans settled
there, and Jewish merchants were attracted by the commercial
advantages of the city (Acts 17:4), although the majority of people made their living by manual labor. Women in Macedonia
enjoyed a higher social position and greater privileges than elsewhere in the civilized world. Second, the city's commercial
activity brought Thessalonica a reputation for evil and licen-
tiousness. The strange mixtures of a seaport city and the rites of
the various cults in the city necessitated a special appeal on the
part of the apostle for chaste living (1 Thess. 4:1–8).

ITS POLITICAL STATUS

Thessalonica was a free city and enjoyed autonomy in all its
internal affairs. Although it was the residence of the provincial
governor, he exercised no civil authority; the city was ruled by
politarchs (cf. Luke's accurate reporting in Acts 17:6). This
political privilege was jealously guarded by the people, who were
extremely sensitive about anything that might result in imperial
disfavor. Therefore, the charge of treason framed against Paul

and his companions was the most dangerous that could have been laid against them in such a city (Acts 17:7).

ITS CULTS

A number of religious cults (with political interrelationships) existed at Thessalonica at the time of Paul. These apparently formed the background for several passages in the letters. The cult of Serapis had a nighttime initiation (see 1 Thess. 5:1–7). The cult of Dionysus offered the hope of a joyous afterlife, symbolized by the phallus. That symbol was sensually provocative and along with the fact that Dionysus was the god of wine and joy gave rise to all kinds of revelry (see 1 Thess. 4:3–8).The female attendants in this cult were referred to as nurses (see 1 Thess. 2:7–8). The cult of Cabirus promised protection for sailors, fertility (symbolized by male genitals), and was considered the nurse and provider of all things (see 1 Thess. 2:7). Other divinities worshiped and referred to include Zeus, Aphrodite, and Demeter.

THE MINISTRY AT THESSALONICA

ITS INITIAL SUCCESS, ACTS 17:1–4

To this city on his second missionary journey came Paul, accompanied by Silas and Timothy. Silas, remember, had been chosen in Antioch as Paul's partner for this second journey after the separation from Barnabas over John Mark. Young Timothy was enlisted at Lystra (Acts 16:1–3) after the journey had begun. After revisiting the churches founded on the first trip, they came to an impasse at Troas until Paul had the vision of the man of Macedonia (northern Greece) calling him to come to Europe to help.

Their first European stop was Philippi, but they were compelled to leave after the illegal imprisonment experience. They then traveled the hundred miles to Thessalonica, where Paul, as was his custom, preached in the synagogue for three Sabbaths with success (Acts 17:2). The converts included Jews and a great

multitude of devout Greeks who were attracted by the mono-
theism and morality of Judaism and who had attached themselves to the synagogue. Some believers were of the upper classes,
but most were apparently of the working class, since Paul
refused to be dependent financially on them in any way.

OPPOSITION AND EXPULSION, ACTS 17:5–9

Naturally, the Jewish community did not like to be depleted
in this manner, so some of the Jews resorted to violence by incit-
ing a mob to attack the house of Jason, Paul's host, and drag
him before the rulers, where he was charged with harboring
traitors to Caesar. This charge of treason is the first recorded
after the trial of Jesus before Pilate and could have been an out-
growth of the eschatological preaching of Paul at Thessalonica
as reflected in the epistles. The politarchs took security of Jason
and the others accused with him and let them go. Probably this
action was in the nature of placing them under a peace bond
that included the guarantee that Paul would leave the city
immediately and not return.

ON TO ATHENS, ACTS 17:10–15

From Thessalonica the missionaries proceeded to Berea, but
soon were compelled to leave there because of opposition from
the Thessalonian Jews who dogged their steps. Paul went on to
Athens, where Timothy joined him and from where he was dispatched back to Thessalonica in order to report on the condition of the young church. Both Timothy and Silas rejoined Paul
at Corinth, from which city the two epistles to the Thessalonians were written (1 Thess. 3:1, 6).

HOW LONG WAS PAUL IN THESSALONICA?

The duration of Paul's stay in Thessalonica is debated. Acts
17:2 declares that he reasoned in the synagogue for three, apparently successive, Sabbaths, while 1 Thessalonians 2:7–11 mentions that he was in Thessalonica long enough to gain employ-

ment. Philippians 4:16 seems to imply he was there long enough to be able to receive two gifts of money from the Philippians.

Because of the apparent teaching of these latter two passages, many think that Paul had to be in Thessalonica over a period of months—certainly longer than three or four weeks. For instance, Ramsay thinks Paul was there six months (Ramsay, *St. Paul the Traveller and the Roman Citizen*, 228). However, the anxious tone of 1 Thessalonians makes clear that Paul was not there long enough to see the church established. Rather, he was forced to leave the city before little more than the work of evangelizing had been done.

As for his working during the stay in the city, this could easily have been necessary even if he stayed only a month and especially if he assumed some or all of the maintenance of Silas and Timothy as well. A careful study of Philippians 4:16 would indicate that the reference probably does not mean Paul received several gifts from the Philippians while at Thessalonica. The verse may be translated this way: "Both [when I was] in Thessalonica and (*kai*) more than once *(hapax kai dis)* [when I was in other places] you sent . . ." (Morris, *The Epistles of Paul to the Thessalonians, 17)*. Thus the verse need not imply that any more than one gift reached Paul in Thessalonica.

So it is possible that Paul was there only about a month. Yet the fact that he must have had a fairly extensive ministry outside the synagogue among Gentiles (see 1 Thess. 1:9) may indicate a ministry of several months in the city.

DATE AND PLACE OF WRITING

As has been stated, both epistles were written from Corinth during the apostle's eighteen-month stay in that city. The first epistle was written during the earlier part of that period, just after Timothy had returned from Thessalonica with news of the progress of the church, and the second letter was dispatched a matter of weeks (or at the most a few months) later. Any date assigned will have to be approximate, though probably the writing of these letters should be placed during the winter of A.D. 51–52. Gallio (Acts 18:12) arrived in Corinth during the summer of 51.

PURPOSES OF FIRST THESSALONIANS

First Thessalonians was written after the receipt of Timothy's favorable report of his visit to the city. Therefore, its first purpose was to express Paul's thanks and give encouragement to the people.

Second, Paul in this epistle defended himself against what was evidently a campaign of the Jewish opponents of Christianity to defame and slander him. They had apparently spread the word that Paul's conduct was dishonorable and that his failure to return to the city proved that he was interested only in whatever profit he could gain from his evangelistic mission in the town. The first three chapters contain Paul's answer to these charges, which may have had some success among the people. Not to have defended himself would have been disastrous to the entire missionary enterprise in all of Macedonia.

A third purpose of the letter was to encourage these new converts to stand fast in the face of persecution and pressure to revert to the easy standards of the paganism from which they had turned.

Fourth, a doctrinal question had arisen in the church concerning the fate of Christians who died before the ushering in of Christ's kingdom. This Paul answers in the fourth chapter.

Finally, some matters in relation to their church life had to be dealt with. Some of the believers needed to be reminded that although Christianity is a religion of charity, they were not to be moochers. In their church services, too, there was some misunderstanding concerning their relationship to the work and gifts of the Holy Spirit and to one another in the congregation.

This is a letter from a pastor who was basically satisfied, even thrilled, with the progress of his flock but who wanted to encourage them to go on in their faith. It is a heartwarming letter showing a side of Paul that we do not see in some of his other epistles.

PURPOSE OF SECOND THESSALONIANS

The purpose of the second epistle can be discovered from the letter itself. In one way or another, information had reached

Paul concerning the state of the church in Thessalonica. Good word came concerning their steadfastness in persecution, and for this Paul commended the believers. However, there had been misapprehension, if not misrepresentation, of the apostle's teaching concerning the coming of the Day of the Lord. Some thought it had evidently begun and that they were experiencing its judgments, whereas he had taught them in the first epistle that they were not appointed unto that wrath. Concerning this, Paul corrected them.

Finally, the brief warning of the first epistle (5:14) against disorderly conduct had had little effect, and the situation had worsened. Concerning this, Paul gave strict and definite instructions. He was careful to give whatever praise was deserved, while at the same time dealing firmly and clearly with the deviations in doctrine and practice.

Some Review Questions

1. Where is Thessalonica? Can you locate it on a map (look for one in the back of your Bible)?
2. On which missionary trip did Paul go to Thessalonica?
3. Where had he come from on that trip before reaching Thessalonica?
4. Where was he when he received the call to go to Greece?
5. How long did Paul and his team stay in Thessalonica?
6. Under what circumstances did he leave the city?
7. When and from where did Paul write 1 Thessalonians?

FIRST THESSALONIANS

OUTLINE OF FIRST THESSALONIANS

SECTION 1: PAUL'S THANKSGIVING FOR AND COMMENDATION OF THE THESSALONIANS (1:1–10)

I. Greetings (1:1)
II. Paul's Thanksgiving for and Commendation of the Thessalonians (1:2–10)
   A. The Content of His Commendation (1:2–8)
      1. Their work of faith (1:3a, 4–5)
      2. Their labor of love (1:3b, 6–8)
         a. The intensity of their labor (1:3b)
         b. The proofs of their labor (1:6–7)
         c. The extent of their labor (1:8)
      3. Their steadfastness of hope (1:3c, 6–7)
   B. The Confirmation of His Commendation (1:9–10)
      1. The Thessalonians' faith confirmed (1:9b)
      2. The Thessalonians' love confirmed (1:9c)
      3. The Thessalonians' hope confirmed (1:10)
         a. The character of their hope
         b. The content of their hope
         c. The center of their hope

SECTION 2: PAUL'S CONDUCT AMONG THE THESSALONIANS (2:1–12)

I. Conduct Characterized by Unselfish Love (2:1–4)
   A. Love of the Truth (2:1–4)
      1. Message proclaimed even in times of suffering and mistreatment (2:2)
      2. Message proclaimed with boldness (2:2)
      3. Message proclaimed with purity (2:3–4)
   B. Love of the Work (2:4)
II. Conduct Characterized by Unstinting Labor (2:5–9)
   A. He labored in Selflessness (2:5–6)
   B. He labored with Gentleness (2:7)
   C. He labored with Willingness (2:8–9)

III. Conduct Characterized by Unspotted Life (2:10–12)
   A. The Excellency of Paul's Life (2:10)
   B. The Example of Paul's Life (2:11–12)

SECTION 3: PAUL'S CONCERN FOR THE THESSALONIANS
(2:13–3:13)

I. Concern That Sufferings Would Hinder Their Progress
(2:13–3:4)
   A. Suffering Because They Received the Gospel as the
   Word of God (2:13–20)
     1. Paul's gratitude for Timothy's report (2:13)
     2. The result of believing (2:14–16)
     3. Paul's reactions (regret and rejoicing) (2:17–20)
   B. Suffering Because of Everyday Opposition Against
   Christians (3:1–4)
     1. Paul's plan to help the Thessalonians (3:1–2a)
     2. Paul's purpose in helping the Thessalonians (3:3a)
     3. Paul's reminder to the Thessalonians (3:3b–4)
II. Concern That Satan Would Tempt the Thessalonians (3:5)
III. Concern About Shortcomings (3:6–13)
   A. The Good Report (3:6–8)
   B. The Continuing Need (3:9–10)
   C. The Cure for Shortcomings (3:11–13)

SECTION 4: INSTRUCTIONS AND EXHORTATIONS
(4:1–5:28)

I. How to Please God (4:1–12)
   A. Exhortation to Abound in Living to Please God (4:1–2)
   B. Exhortation to Be Sanctified (4:3a)
   C. Exhortation to Sexual Purity (4:3b–8)
     1. The meaning of immorality (4:3b)
     2. The means of experiencing sexual purity: properly
     "possessing one's vessel" (4:4)
     3. The consequences of immorality (4:5–8)

    D. Exhortation to Brotherly Love (4:9–10)
       1. The explanation of love (4:9)
       2. The extent of love (4:10)
       3. The expression of love (4:10)
       4. The expansion of love (4:10)
    E. Exhortation to Have Correct Ambitions (4:11–12)
II. Instruction Concerning the Rapture of Living Believers and the Resurrection of Believers Who Have Died (4:13–18)
    A. We Have a Preview (4:13–14)
    B. We Have a Promise (4:15)
    C. We Have a Picture (4:16–18)
       1. A return (4:16)
       2. A resurrection (4:16)
       3. A rapture (4:17)
       4. A reunion (4:17)
       5. A reassurance (4:18)
III. Instruction and Exhortation Concerning the Day of the Lord (5:1–11)
    A. A Definition of the Day of the Lord
    B. The Relation of the Day of the Lord to the Rapture of the Church (5:1)
    C. The Beginning of the Day of the Lord (5:2–3)
    D. The Exhortations to Believers in Light of the Coming of the Day of the Lord (5:4–11)
       1. Remember you are all sons of light (5:4–5)
       2. Don't be asleep, watch, be sober (5:6–8)
       3. Be encouraged (5:9–11)
IV. Instructions Concerning Various Responsibilities in the Church (5:12–24)
    A. Instructions for Those Who Are Led by Leaders in the Church (5:12–13)
    B. Instructions for Those Who Lead (5:12–13)
    C. Instructions for the Entire Group (5:14–15)
       1. Warn the unruly (5:14a)
       2. Comfort the fainthearted (5:14b)
       3. Help the weak (5:14c)
       4. Be long-suffering toward all (5:14d)
       5. Do not render evil for evil (5:15a)

6. Follow that which is good (5:15b)
7. Always rejoice (5:16)
8. Be prayerful (5:17)
9. Be thankful (5:18)
10. Do not quench the Spirit (5:19)
11. Do not despise prophesyings (5:20)
12. Examine, or prove, everything (5:21–22)
13. Be sanctified (5:23–24)
V. Conclusion (5:25–28)

1
GREETINGS, THANKSGIVING, AND COMMENDATION

1:1–10

SECTION 1: PAUL'S THANKSGIVING FOR AND COMMENDATION OF THE THESSALONIANS, 1:1–10

First-century letters began sensibly. Instead of requiring the reader to look at the end to find the signature, they began with the name of the writer, the name of the recipient, and some sort of greeting. First Thessalonians is no exception.

It is always interesting to observe how Paul introduces himself to the various churches and individuals to whom he writes. Sometimes he designates himself as an apostle (Gal. 1:1), sometimes as a servant (Rom. 1:1), but here without any additional descriptive word. He does, however, associate himself with Silas and Timothy (the latter appears in ten of Paul's epistles), not as coauthors but as a matter of courtesy since they were with Paul during the ministry in Thessalonica. The name *Paul* means "little" and was the Roman name given him at birth along with his Jewish name, Saul. It was common practice among the Jews to give a child both a Jewish and a Gentile name, and particularly would this have been natural with Paul, whose father was a Roman citizen. The Jewish name, Saul, is used until his ministry turns to the Gentiles (Acts 13:9), after which his Gentile name, Paul, is appropriately used.

After being forced to leave Thessalonica, Paul and Silas went to Berea (Timothy was probably with them, though he may have joined them later, Acts 17:14). After they all met at Athens, Paul sent Timothy back to Thessalonica (1 Thess. 3:2) and Silas to Macedonia, likely to Philippi, because Paul feared that the persecution might have spread there. Then all three met again at Corinth (Acts 18:5).

The recipients of the letter are designated as the "church of the Thessalonians." The form of address is unique, for usually Paul says "to the church in such and such a place." The difference emphasizes his individual interest in each member of this church. The position of these believers, while locally in Thessalonica and circumstantially in persecution, was spiritually in God the Father and the Lord Jesus Christ. The oneness of the Father and the Son as well as the oneness of believers with the Godhead is affirmed.

Paul's greeting is "Grace be unto you, and peace" (the remainder of the verse as found in the King James Version is absent from better manuscripts). Grace, akin to the word *joy,* is that which causes joy, and in a Christian sense it means the undeserved favor of God toward the sinner in providing the free gift of salvation through the death of Christ. To us today, peace means the absence of war; but in the Old Testament it meant harmony between man and God and the resultant wholeness and prosperity of the soul. As used here, it of course has that Old Testament flavor with the Christian additive that the harmony was made possible through the death of Christ. The order of the two words is significant, for there can be no real peace until grace has been experienced in the heart.

THE CONTENT OF HIS COMMENDATION, 1:2–8

It was also conventional in ancient letters to open with a word of gratitude. Paul's commendation of his readers, however, is not a matter of following convention, but it is a genuine expression of his feeling for them (cf. Gal. 1:6, where there is no such commendation) and an attempt to raise their thoughts to God on whom was their dependence. The regularity of his thanksgiving for them (as expressed in the words "always" and "without ceasing" KJV) also shows that this was no mere perfunctory matter with him. Paul was practicing what he preached when he prayed for them "without ceasing" (this is the same word used in 5:17). The three particular things for which Paul was thankful form the content of the rest of the chapter.

THEIR WORK OF FAITH, 1:3a, 4–5

The first of the three things for which Paul gives thanks is the work of faith. This refers to the initial act of faith, which brought salvation to the Thessalonians, and it also includes the works that followed that initial act of saving faith. Because the Thessalonians' faith exhibited itself in good works, Paul was certain that they belonged to God's elect. They were those who were beloved of God. The word *beloved* is a perfect participle, which means that God's love existed in the past and continues on to the present with unabated force.

Election proceeds from this love of God for His chosen ones (notice the same connection between election, or selection, and God's love in Eph. 1:4–5). It also is the work of a sovereign or supreme God (Rom. 9:11), occurring before the foundation of the world (Eph. 1:4) and involving the ministry of the Holy Spirit (2 Thess. 2:13), the message through a messenger (Rom. 10:14, 17) and personal faith (2 Thess. 2:13). "This is the work of God, that you believe in Him [Jesus Christ] whom He has sent" (John 6:29). There need be no fear, only awe, in considering the doctrine of election, for if God could not have elected His people out of His sovereign love, none of us would have been saved.

It is sometimes said that one cannot know whether or not another is elect, but here Paul claims that very knowledge. His reasons are stated in verse 5, and they are based on the way the Gospel came to the Thessalonians during his evangelistic mission in their city. Verse 5 begins with "for" ("because"). There are three reasons that Paul knew the Thessalonians were among

God's elect. The first is negative—"not . . . in word only"; that is, not in any power that could come through the eloquence of speech. By contrast, the second characteristic is that it did come in power. Evidently Paul is not referring to miracles accompanying the preaching of the Gospel at Thessalonica (this would require the use of the plural of the word *power*) but to the sincerity and simplicity of the message as empowered by the Holy Spirit. Words, however eloquent, cannot change man's heart, but the Spirit using the preached message can and does (cf. John 16:7–11). The third characteristic of the work of faith was that it brought to the three missionaries complete assurance of the effectiveness of the message they had preached. "Much assurance" (KJV) is closely connected with the Holy Spirit (for there is no repetition of "in" before "much assurance") and means the confidence in the message that the Spirit brought to both the evangelists and the converts. For confirmation of what he has just asserted concerning his preaching, Paul appeals in the last part of verse 5 to his readers' knowledge of the truth of what he has just written.

THEIR LABOR OF LOVE, 1:3b, 6–8

The second thing for which the apostle commends his readers is their labor of love.

The intensity of their labor, 1:3. The word Paul uses for labor in verse 3 means "fatiguing work" and differs from work in the phrase *work of faith* in that it includes the cost associated with the labor.

The proofs of their labor, 1:6–7. They performed their labor of love in spite of "affliction." The word in verse 6 means severe difficulties, not simply discomfort. Becoming a Christian does not guarantee a trouble-free life.

The extent of their labor, 1:8. Love is that which seeks the highest good for the one loved, and since the greatest good one can do for an unredeemed person is to bring him the Gospel, a labor of love would mean the sounding out of the word of the Lord. This the Thessalonians did to the point of fatigue (cf. Rev.

14:13) in Macedonia, Achaia, and every place (v. 8). The word translated "sounded out" is picturesque. The Greek letters simply changed into English characters spell our word *echo*. Thus the picture is of the message of the Gospel so stirring the strings of the Thessalonians' hearts that it reverberated in strong and clear tones to all Greece and everywhere. That which was sounded out was the word of the Lord, a phrase that is "used here with direct reference to the Gospel-message ("a word having the Lord for its origin, its centre, and its end')" (Milligan, *St.Paul's Epistles to the Thessalonians*, 12). The exact phrase is used elsewhere by Paul with the same meaning only in 2 Thessalonians 3:1. This is the only church Paul calls a pattern, not only to the pagans but to other Christians, for to labor in sending forth the Gospel is the greatest work of love anyone can perform.

THEIR STEADFASTNESS OF HOPE, 1:3c, 6–7

The third thing for which the converts are commended is their steadfastness of hope. This word in verse 3 is *hupomone*, which does not denote a negative and passive resignation to persecution or problems, but rather a positive and optimistic fortitude in spite of indignities suffered. The Christian's confident expectation is in his Lord and particularly in the return of the Lord. This same idea concerning our hope is emphasized in the first chapter of the second epistle.

Such hope always shines brightest in the midst of persecution, and the Thessalonians knew much about this even in their short Christian experience. They had been under such pressure and affliction that Paul likened their case to his own and to the Lord's (v. 6). But their suffering was accompanied by joy inspired by or originating from the Holy Spirit (the genitive "of the Holy Spirit" is that of source—a joy that comes from the Spirit). The Christian is never promised a bed of roses (see John 16:33), but even in affliction he may always experience joy that the Holy Spirit brings to his heart (cf. John 16:22).

Because of this, the Thessalonians became examples to other believers in Greece (v. 7). The word "example" is *tupos*, from which we get the English word *type*. It originally meant the mark of a blow (cf. John 20:25); then it came to mean the figure formed by the blow; and thus its resultant meaning is "image," or "pattern" (Heb. 8:5). The meaning, then, is that the conduct of these believers served as a pattern for other Christians in the two provinces of Greece: Macedonia (the northern part of Greece, of which Thessalonica was the chief city) and Achaia (the southern part of Greece, of which Corinth, the place of the writing of the letter, was the principal city).

THE CONFIRMATION OF HIS COMMENDATION, 1:9–10

Paul makes a very daring statement in verse 9. He says in effect that anybody (both Christian and pagan) could tell what was going on in Thessalonica, so active was the group there. It was not merely a matter of the missionaries' commending the church, but anyone you might ask would say the same thing.

THE THESSALONIANS' FAITH CONFIRMED, 1:9b

Their faith was confirmed by those around them who continually (the verb "show" [see KJV] is present tense) testified to the fact that these Christians were different because they had turned to God from idols. The phrase "turned to God" also shows that the majority of the church were from a Gentile, not a Jewish, background.

THE THESSALONIANS' LOVE CONFIRMED, 1:9c

Their labor of love in disseminating the Gospel is confirmed in the phrase "to serve the living and true God"(KJV). "Serve" really means to serve as a slave, and the Old Testament picture of the perpetual bondslave is in Deuteronomy 15:16ff. In our Lord's humiliation, He took "the form of a bond-servant" (Phil. 2:7), and Paul too delights to call himself a slave of Jesus Christ (Rom. 1:1). Truly these Thessalonians did become followers of him and of the Lord (v. 6) in willing slavery to Christ, their Master.

THE THESSALONIANS' HOPE CONFIRMED, 1:10

The character of their hope. That patient endurance of hope is expressed in verse 10 by the word "wait." Actually the Greek word is a compound of the usual word for *wait* preceded by a preposition that intensifies the idea but which also means *up*, when standing by itself. In English we might capture that intensive meaning by actually translating the preposition as part of the meaning of the verb. Thus the meaning is: They were waiting up for their Lord. Do you not see the outlook of expectancy, triumphant hope, and constant endurance displayed in the attitude of waiting up?

The content of their hope. Their waiting up was for a person, and as Christians we wait not so much for an event as for a person.

The center of their hope. That person for whom we wait up is identified in three ways. He is the Son, the divine One. He is Jesus, the human One. He is the deliverer from the wrath to come, and that deliverance is complete, for it is out of *(ek)* the coming wrath.

This was the report of those who lived with the believers and who watched their lives day by day, as well as those who lived in distant regions and heard of their witness secondhand. It is a convincing testimony to the power of the Gospel to change lives, which power has not diminished over the centuries and which testimony ought to be just as clear today.

SOME REVIEW QUESTIONS

1. Think of some specific afflictions believers whom you know are experiencing.
2. Are you someone whose Christian walk should be imitated?
3. Without radio, TV, tapes, videos, books, the Internet, etc., how could verse 8 have been accomplished?
4. What is the wrath to come (see Rev. 6:12–17)?

2

PAUL'S UNSELFISH LOVE

2:1–4

SECTION 2: PAUL'S CONDUCT AMONG THE THESSALONIANS, 2:1–12

Paul now returns to the subject he briefly touched on in the last part of 1:5, his conduct during the mission in Thessalonica. He appeals to his readers to affirm the truth of what he is going to say in this chapter. The word *yourselves* is in an emphatic position in the Greek sentence. He calls on them to testify that his entrance among them did not prove to be in vain (from *kene,* "empty, void of power"). This is a daring thing for a man to do, for Paul is saying in effect, "Ask anybody in Thessalonica; they'll tell you that I'm telling the truth when I say that I behaved holily and justly all the time I was in the city." In these first twelve verses lies the secret of Paul's success as a servant of Christ. One might title this section "Successful Service" or "A Winning Witness."

CONDUCT CHARACTERIZED BY UNSELFISH LOVE, 2:1–4 LOVE OF THE TRUTH, 2:3

Paul's conduct did not include any love of self or of personal comforts.

MESSAGE PROCLAIMED
EVEN IN TIMES OF SUFFERING AND MISTREATMENT, 2:2

To prove this, he cites what happened to him and his group at Philippi (Acts 16:13, 19, 23, 37). There they had been subjected to both physical suffering and mental torture ("mistreated"), for they had undergone the affliction of beating and imprisonment, and they had endured indignities from which Roman citizens were exempt. It was unlawful to strip, beat, and imprison Roman citizens without a hearing, but in spite of the fact that this had happened to Paul at Philippi, and in spite of the fact that it might have happened again at Thessalonica, that did not deter him from preaching the truth in Thessalonica.

MESSAGE PROCLAIMED WITH BOLDNESS, 2:2

Boldness is a compound of two words that mean "all speech." Therefore, basically it means freedom of speech and the resultant confidence that comes from such freedom (cf. Acts 26:26; Eph. 3:12). This boldness does not result from mere natural courage but from supernatural enablement, for it is "boldness in our God."

MESSAGE PROCLAIMED WITH PURITY, 2:3–4

Paul's conduct among them was absolutely pure and approved of God. The fact that Paul evidently found it necessary to mention this implies that he had been charged with deceptive conduct. It was not uncommon for preachers of strange cults to seek only their own financial profit, and apparently Paul had been classed as one of those.

Paul could boldly exhort people to receive the Gospel of God for three reasons.

1. First, he was assured that the Gospel did not have its source in error ("not of deceit" (KJV)—*plane* means "error," not "deceit). The early missionaries of the Cross knew that they were not victims of a great deception or

lie. The facts and purpose of Christ's life, death, and resurrection were and are true.

2. Second, the secret of the Gospel was not in its appeal to uncleanness. It may seem strange to us to realize that Paul felt it necessary to disclaim sensuality, but the success of heathen religions could often be traced to their sanction of immorality. Paul's message had evidently been charged with such, and he makes clear that Christianity did not require licentious rites in order to promote it as the cults did.

3. Third, the sending of the truth was not with impure motives. Paul loved the truth, because it did not require guile to convince. The word *guile* (KJV) is from a word meaning "bait" and thus signifies any crafty design or catching. The preposition here is different from that in the preceding two phrases. The source of Paul's exhortation was not from *(ek)* error nor from *(ek)* uncleanness, nor was it in *(en)* the atmosphere of deceit. Who can help loving a message like this? And yet it is this very love that many Christians do not have, and that is why they find it difficult to witness.

LOVE OF THE WORK, 2:4

Not only did Paul love and preach the truth, but he also loved the work. This is proved by the fact that he had been approved of God over the years. The word translated "approved" means "to prove" and thus "approve." It is in the perfect tense, which shows that Paul is referring to the entire span of his Christian life up to this time. He was approved of God during his three years of seclusion in Arabia (Gal. 1:16–17). He continued to be tested and approved during the seven or eight years he had to spend in Tarsus after returning from Arabia (cf. Acts 9:30; 11:25). This must have been very difficult for the Christian man who had left home some twenty years before to study under Gamaliel in Jerusalem to become a rabbi.

He proved himself further on the first missionary journey through disappointment (when John Mark left the party, Acts

13:13), danger (when he was stoned at Lystra, Acts 14:19), and dispute (at the Jerusalem council, Acts 15). In all the tests God had given him, he had proved himself faithful and could therefore speak in this confident manner of God's approval on his ministry. In this assurance of past approval Paul was speaking to the Thessalonians (present tense).

Too, it was because he realized that it is God who gives approval that he did not aim his ministry at pleasing men but God who "examines" (this is the same word as translated "approved" in the first part of the verse) the heart. It is always a temptation to gear our message to that which pleases men and to aim our methods at that which will not displease them in any way. This Paul did not do. Remember, blessing on the message is promised (Isa. 55:11), but approval of the messenger is earned.

3
PAUL'S UNSTINTING LABOR

2:5–9

CONDUCT CHARACTERIZED BY UNSTINTING LABOR, 2:5–9

HE LABORED IN SELFLESSNESS, 2:5–6

Paul's unselfish labor at Thessalonica was characterized as being free from three things. (1) It was free from undue influence. The sense of the word translated "flattering" is difficult to convey, for it has the idea of using the kind of acceptable speech that lulls another person into a false sense of security in order that the speaker may gain his own ends. Our English word *cajolery* is similar. (2) It was free from covetousness and greed. "Pretext" means "cloak"; that is, Paul did not put on a cloak or mask to try to cover up his real motive of greed. He did not seek from his converts anything unfairly.

Covetousness is not only the desire for money but for self-promotion, and this Paul emphatically disclaims in his evangelizing of Thessalonica. Indeed, he explains later on (v. 9) how he labored in order to give the Gospel to them freely. To attest this, he appeals to God as his witness, since it was impossible for his readers to see what was in his heart. He is claiming more than that his actions were free from covetousness; his heart was free from such, too, and God bore him witness in that. (3) It was free from self-glory, though as an apostle he could have asserted his authority. To glorify is to manifest or show off. Paul disclaims that he ever sought that men should show him off. Paul has obtained honor of men, but he never looked for praise from men.

HE LABORED WITH GENTLENESS, 2:7

Rather than trying to make gain from the Thessalonians, Paul and his companions were gentle among them. The exact reading of v. 7 is difficult to determine. The word "gentle" *(epioi)* is spelled in Greek exactly the same way as the word "babe" *(nepioi)* with the exception of the first letter, which also happens to be the last letter of the preceding word. The manuscript evidence gives some preference to "babe," while "gentle" seems to make better sense. Since the evidence is fairly evenly divided, and since it is not difficult to account for altering the original either way, it is not easy to choose between "we were gentle" and "we were babes." In either case, the preachers treated the people with tenderness and without any trace of superiority.

Concerning the figure of a nurse cherishing her children, there is no manuscript question. Since children are "her own children" (the reflexive pronoun is in the text), most likely the nurse is also the mother, and thus we should understand the word "nurse" to mean "nursing mother." Her action is one of cherishing, or caring for, her children with extreme tenderness. The word for "cherish" means "to warm" and is used of the way a mother bird covers her young (Deut. 22:6); its only other occurrence in the New Testament is of our Lord's relationship to His church (Eph. 5:29). Warm—don't scald—people with the truth. This picture which Paul paints of his labors is very vivid and evidently in sharp contrast to the one his opponents were slanderously ascribing to him.

HE LABORED WITH WILLINGNESS, 2:8–9

Utmost willingness also characterized the ministry in Thessalonica.

(1) To give the Gospel to the Thessalonians. Paul yearned to see them saved (the word for "affectionately desirous" [KJV] is rare and probably means a mother's yearning over her child. See the Septuagint of Job 3:12 for the only other occurrence).

(2) To give his life for them. Such strong motivation brought continuous willingness (the verb is in the imperfect tense, signifying continuousness) to give everything ("our own souls" KJV) for their converts. It was the unreserved abandonment which was the secret of Paul's effectiveness.

(3) To give his ministry freely to them.

There was no holding back of anything, and he asked the Thessalonians to remember that he worked night and day in order that he could support himself and his party financially and give the Gospel to them without charge. Undoubtedly, some of the chief women of the city and perhaps Jason too had money, and we know that the church in Philippi sent Paul money later on (cf. Phil. 4:16); nevertheless, during the period of evangelization he would not receive their financial support. Every Jewish boy was taught a trade; likely Paul used his trade, tentmaking, to support himself in Thessalonica as he did elsewhere (Acts 18:3; 20:34). No one could charge him with greed. This is the secret of Paul's success—the continual and selfless giving of his all to people whom he loved dearly.

4

PAUL'S UNSPOTTED LIFE

2:10–12

CONDUCT CHARACTERIZED BY UNSPOTTED LIFE, 2:10–12

THE EXCELLENCY OF PAUL'S LIFE, 2:10

Paul now speaks of the unspotted testimony of his own life, and since it was a matter of both inward and outward observation, he calls both his readers and God to witness the truth of what he is about to claim. Although some commentators have emphasized that "devoutly" refers to Paul's conduct in relation to God, "uprightly" in relation to man, and "blamelessly" in relation to self, it seems better to recognize the three adverbs as describing fully the apostle's conduct and character in all his relationships. This must have been a true and accurate description of Paul's character and conduct; otherwise, he would not have called so confidently on the believers to affirm his testimony.

THE EXAMPLE OF PAUL'S LIFE, 2:11–12

Paul's excellent life serves for all of us as an example, exhortation, and encouragement to live continually in a manner that pleases our Lord. This is always the standard for all believers everywhere and in every age. Paul reminds the believers how paternally he dealt with them. The figure of a paternal relationship with believers appears only in Paul's epistles and only in connection with the conversion experience (cf. 1 Cor. 4:14; 2 Cor. 6:13; Gal. 4:19; Philem. 10). Like a father, Paul was careful and wise in his dealings with these young Christians. He exhorted them, which shows the earnestness of his appeal. He comforted them, which shows that he was not unmindful of their particularly trying circumstances and was, as a result, sensible in his exhortation. He charged them with firmness and without compromise. But there was a tender definiteness in all his dealings with them.

Before leaving this section, we need to be reminded of what Paul declared in verse 1—the proof that his ministry at Thessalonica was not empty was the testimony of his converts. It was not a case of the preacher's building himself up in the eyes of the people; it was a case of the people's gladly and fully affirming the effectiveness of the preacher's ministry among them. It is easy to do the former; it is rare to experience the latter. May God give us more Christian workers in our day who will give themselves unselfishly and unstintingly to the work.

SOME REVIEW QUESTIONS

1. What kind of mistreatment did Paul experience at Philippi (2:2)? Be specific and detailed.
2. Should pastors and missionaries support themselves or be supported by others?
3. List the characteristics of Paul's ministry in Thessalonica from 2:3–11.
4. Four times in this section Paul uses the word "gospel." Can you explain the Gospel clearly, yet completely, in about twenty-five words?

5

CONCERN THAT SUFFERINGS WOULD HINDER THEIR PROGRESS

2:13–3:4

SECTION 3: PAUL'S CONCERN FOR THE THESSALONIANS, 2:13–3:13

In this section we catch a glimpse of Paul's concern for the church. It should be remembered how Paul and his companions were forced to leave the city before they had had much time to ground the young church. For this reason he had been anxious about the welfare of the group and had sent Timothy from Athens to ascertain their spiritual state. A good report came back, and Paul was greatly encouraged. But in this section we discover what was on the apostle's heart, and it is plain that his concern was in the realm of spiritual things and not in the area of material lacks. And it is still true today that God's people should be chiefly concerned not about new facilities but about the spiritual state of the group.

Suffering Because They Received the Gospel as the Word of God, 2:13-20

Paul's Gratitude for Timothy's Report, 2:13

Paul first expresses the concern he had lest the persecutions that the young church had to endure had shaken their faith. The report from Timothy had assured him that such was not the case and he gives thanks for that (v. 13). "For this reason" (v. 13) refers to what follows in the paragraph. The fact that they had not defected proved that the Thessalonians had received the missionaries' message as the word of God. Paul's preaching was with conviction, for he believed that what he said was not of his own devising but was the word of God Himself. Twice he employs the phrase in this single verse.

The second occurrence is especially emphatic—"you accepted it not as the word of men, but for what it really is, the word of God." He also claims for the word an effective, productive operation simply because it works in the heart of the believer (or is "made to work," passive, as some think. The phrase "word of hearing" reminds us that the message was delivered orally, not in written form. It was from God but spoken through human beings and requires faith to receive.

The Result of Believing, 2:14–16

Believers may expect to be opposed by unbelievers. So the result of the Thessalonians' stand and activity for Christ brought immediate persecution. The details are lacking, but the fact of it is clearly stated in Acts 17. The Gentile converts at Thessalonica had suffered from their fellow Gentiles (because the Jews in the city had aroused them by appealing to their political passions and loyalties) just as the Christian Jews in Judea had suffered from their fellow Jews. (Paul himself had contributed to the sufferings of those churches in Judea.)

Their cases were identical. Both Paul and Silas (Acts 15:22) belonged to the church in Jerusalem and likely related to the Thessalonians the history of persecution there. "Countrymen" refers to Gentiles in Thessalonica who persecuted the church there, though Jews were also involved. Jews could not tolerate Gentiles coming to know the living and true God without first becoming proselytes to Judaism. It was Jews who attacked the church in Judea, who killed the Lord Jesus (Acts 4:27), who killed the prophets (such as Stephen, whom the Jews killed, Acts 6:9), and who drove Paul out of Thessalonica (literally, "chased him out," v. 15).

At Thessalonica, however, things had not gotten to the point of martyrdom. Paul himself had experienced more than his share of persecution, as the Jews dogged his trail trying to forbid him to preach the Gospel. The truth of verse 16 was illustrated in Paul's life at Antioch (Acts 13:45, 50), Iconium (Acts 14:1–5), Lystra (Acts 14:19), Berea (Acts 17:13), Corinth (Acts 18:12), and, of course, Thessalonica. But through it all, Paul and the Thessalonian believers remained steadfast and true to their calling as Christians. As a result, the enemies of Christ "fill up the measure of their sins" (v. 16) like filling a cup to the brim with sins (the compound *anapleroo* implies a full measure, that is, to the brim).

Paul is saying that God allows His people to be persecuted sometimes in order to prove the evil nature of man and show the righteous character of His judgment when it comes (cf. Gen. 15:16; Dan. 8:23; Matt. 23:32; Rev. 6:17). God allows the wicked to fill their evil deeds full in order to demonstrate to all that His judgments are righteous ones whenever they come, whether in this life or after. Thus, God's purpose is at work, too, in permitting suffering.

PAUL'S REACTIONS (REGRET AND REJOICING), 2:17–20

This victory on the part of the believers was in spite of their being orphaned (this is the word translated "taken away" in v. 17) of their spiritual father, Paul. The expressions of bereavement in verse 17, which his departure caused, the repeated statements of attempts to go to them in verse 18, and the expressions of esteem in verse 19 all give the lie to any possible accusation Paul's enemies may have brought against him that he quickly lost inter-

est in his converts or that he fled because of the attacks made. In
fact, he was forced out of the city (passive voice in v. 17 referring
to Acts 17:9). Paul's "short while" had been extended longer
than he expected, which intensified his feeling of bereavement
(vv. 17–18). Satan can hinder (v. 18) and so can God (Acts
16:6–7). Through it all, Paul continued to have deep love for
those converts, looking ahead to the time when they would all be
united and receive crowns for their work (vv. 19–20).They were
to him his hope, joy, and crown of rejoicing at the coming of the
Lord. Paul served with the coming of Christ in view.

SUFFERING BECAUSE OF EVERYDAY
OPPOSITION AGAINST CHRISTIANS, 3:1–4

PAUL'S PLAN TO HELP THE THESSALONIANS, 3:1–2a

The chapter division is unfortunate here. The "therefore"
links this to the preceding section. Because of having to leave his
converts, and because he had himself been hindered from returning to the city, Paul could scarcely bear up under the silence and
uncertainty of not knowing how the believers were doing. Therefore, he sent Timothy back to see how the young church was faring. The "we" in verse 1 indicates that Timothy concurred with
the plan. Paul was willing to do this in spite of the fact that it
meant that he would be left alone in Athens. Evidently Silas was
still ministering in Berea and had not yet rejoined the party. All
three met again in Corinth, where the letter was written. As much
as Paul loved the Thessalonians, he hated to see Timothy leave
him, for he used a word that literally means "abandon" (cf. Mark
12:19; Eph. 5:31). It is reenforced by the use of "alone" (v. 1),
showing the sense of desolation that overcame Paul in Athens as
he faced the philosophers of that city (Acts 17:22–32). Even ministers of the Gospel feel depressed and alone at times.

However, it was important that Timothy go. He is called by
three terms of endearment—"brother," "servant" (RSV) (cf. 1 Tim.
4:6 for the only other time it is used of Timothy), and "fellow
worker" (though this is not in some texts). The word for "servant" is not the word that means "slave" but the word from

which we get the term "deacon." It is used here in the nontechnical sense of one who renders service, and not in the technical sense of an official deacon, a church officer. Timothy's service to the Thessalonian church on this occasion was twofold. He was to establish them. The word contains the idea of strengthening and is from a root meaning "a support." He was also to comfort them, but that word has more meaning than simply a neutral soothing of them in their difficulties. It also means encouraging or helping them positively for the battle that faced them.

PAUL'S PURPOSE IN HELPING THE THESSALONIANS, 3:3a

Paul had reiterated to the Thessalonians when he was with them (the verb is imperfect in v. 4 and shows repeated telling) that persecution was to be expected. Therefore, he expected them to realize that the cure for sufferings was not relief from them, and that no one should be moved away from his commitment to Christ by persecution (v. 3). The word "moved" (KJV) is used outside the New Testament of a dog wagging its tail and therefore comes to have the sense of "to fawn upon" or "to flatter." Thus Paul is saying that Timothy's job was to show the believers that they should not yield to flattery in the midst of testings. Undoubtedly, some of the Jews were urging them to reject Christianity and turn to Judaism, but Paul was emphatically warning them that this would not cure their sufferings. Yielding to such flattery might instead lead to compromise or even to abandoning their faith.

PAUL'S REMINDER TO THE THESSALONIANS, 3:3b–4

He further reminded the believers through Timothy that they should remember that affliction is the normal lot of a Christian and should not be regarded as something unusual or strange. We are appointed to such. "Appoint" (KJV) is a strong word used, for instance, of a city set on a hill (Matt. 5:14) or of being set for the defense of the Gospel (Phil. 1:16). Sufferings are by divine appointment, and remembering this truth along with steadfastness is what is needed in times of stress.

6

CONCERN THAT
SATAN WOULD TEMPT

3:5

Paul now reasserts his concern for the Christians as he did in verse 1. However, here there is greater emphasis on his personal concern for them as evidenced by the use of the singular in contrast to the plural in verse 1. His concern was for their faith— that it was standing the test of time in the midst of the temptations of Satan. Here the devil is presented in his characteristic role of tempter (cf. Matt. 4:3; 6:13; Mark 1:13; 1 Cor. 7:5). The indicative mood, which Paul uses in the phrase "lest by some means the tempter have tempted you" (KJV), shows that he was certain that the tempting had taken place—it was already a fact. However, the use of the subjunctive in the phrase "and our labour be in vain" makes that a matter of doubt. In other words, he is sure that Satan has been tempting, but he does not think that the Thessalonians had been yielding. If they had, then his hard work would have indeed been in vain, but he doubts that such was the case.

There is a time break between verses 5 and 6, for Timothy had completed his trip to Thessalonica and had rejoined Paul at Corinth.

7
CONCERN ABOUT
SHORTCOMINGS

3:6–13

THE GOOD REPORT, 3:6–8

When Timothy returned from Thessalonica he brought with him a good report of the steadfastness of the believers (v. 6). This meant so much to Paul that he calls it "good news," literally "a gospel." It concerned the Thessalonians' faith (toward God) and love (toward people). "Faith" here does not refer to the initial act of believing but to their Christian growth.

Particularly, their love for Paul himself had not waned in his absence. That remembrance of him was good, that is, kindly or well disposed; it was continuous—always; and it was reciprocal. Again we see Paul's tender love and concern for his converts. This good report brought comfort and life itself to Paul (vv. 7–8). Their faith, love, and longing comforted the apostle. The word "comfort" means more than soothing; it means "strengthening," and it came to Paul at a time when he needed it, for he was in the midst of the pressure of affliction and distress. Both words imply trouble from without—"affliction" meaning "choking, pressing care," and "distress" signifying the crushing kind of trouble.

It is easy to see why he speaks of his situation in such terms, for he was at Athens alone and had just suffered four successive experiences of apparent defeat since he set foot in Europe. At Philippi he had been cast in jail and asked to leave the city. At Thessalonica he had been forced to leave and to guarantee that he would not return. At Berea he was pursued by the Jews and compelled to move on. At Athens he had had little success with the philosophers of the city. Surely he was in afflictions and distress, and this news meant strength and life to him. It brought to him a revival of energy that was not a passing thing but a continual source of inspiration (note the present tense of "we live" in v. 8 KJV). The construction of the clause "if ye stand fast in the Lord" (KJV) is unusual, for the indicative is used, whereas this particular word for "if" usually takes the subjunctive. It "gives a touch of definiteness" (Morris, *The Epistles of Paul to the Thessalonians*, 67) and shows that Paul did not really have misgivings about their standing fast.

THE CONTINUING NEED, 3:9–10

Because of this good report, Paul expresses his thanksgiving for the Thessalonians (v. 9). Such thanksgiving is actually due God, for the doubly compounded (with *anti* and *apo*) verb *antapodounai* ("render again" KJV) "shows that the thanksgiving is not really *giving* but *paying;* it is rendering what is due" (Plummer, *A Commentary on St. Paul's First Epistle to the Thessalonian,* 50). But, though Paul is grateful, he is not satisfied, for he continually made supplication (*deomenoi,* a stronger word than the simple *proseuchesthai,* "pray") in order that he might see them again and have a part in their spiritual growth (v. 10). This prayer was intense, for Paul joins to the phrase "night and day" the adverb "exceedingly" (KJV). This is a very strong word, found in the New Testament elsewhere only in 1 Thessalonians 5:13 and Ephesians 3:20. This is also a doubly compounded word (with *huper* and *ek*) meaning "very, very exceedingly."

This prayer was not answered until some years later when Paul returned to Macedonia (Acts 20:1–2), but he longed to perfect them. "Perfect" (KJV) means to render complete, as one might repair fishing nets (Matt. 4:21) or restore fallen saints (Gal. 6:1) or equip believers for ministry (Eph. 4:12). The Thessalonians needed this ministry in order to supply that which was lacking in their faith. Paul did not consider that the Great Commission had been fulfilled only when people were saved. He realized that there also had to be the work of building them up so that their faith would not be defective in any way. His great pastor's heart shows itself again in this verse.

THE CURE FOR SHORTCOMINGS, 3:11–13

Paul now prays for the believers in order that they might be made complete in their faith. His first petition is that he might be brought to them. It would be God and Christ who would do this. It is important to notice that "our Lord Jesus Christ" is linked with "God himself" (KJV) as closely as possible, and furthermore that the verb is singular. There could scarcely be a clearer way of emphasizing the deity of Christ and His equality with the Father. The verb "direct" means "make straight" as in Luke 1:79 and indicates a removing of the obstacles Satan had put in Paul's way (cf. 2:18).

The second petition is that the Thessalonians might abound in love toward one another and all men (v. 12). The purpose of this is stated in verse 13. It is in order that God might establish them in holiness. The word "heart" indicates the whole personality as in 2:4 and James 5:8. The holiness spoken of here is the resulting state of sanctification that is the result of the process of sanctification. In the Septuagint it is used only of God and thus connotes a high state. Abounding love would establish them unblamable in the state of being set apart to God. God Himself is the standard, and holiness is "before God" (KJV). This idea is reinforced by mentioning the appearance of Christ at His return with the "holy ones" (NIV). The phrase can mean "saints" who accompany Christ as in 4:14 (Findlay, *The Epistles of Paul the Apostle to the Thessalonians,* 76), or it can mean "angels" as taught in Mark 8:38 (Plummer, *A Commen-*

tary on St. Paul's First Epistle to the Thessalonians, 54), or it may include both, which is likely here.

Throughout this section, which has been dealing with causes for concern in the life of the church, we find indications of how to strengthen believers in order that sufferings, Satan, or shortcomings will not hinder their growth and maturing. For one thing, the work of the ministers of Christ is an important factor in keeping the church growing and healthy (2:17–20; 3:2). This is exemplified by the ministries of Paul and Timothy. For another thing, we see the importance of prayer in the life and growth of the church (3:11–13). Finally, we see the need for knowledge of the truth of God as recorded in the Bible in order to appraise correctly the events of life. This is exemplified in the matter of realizing that suffering is the appointed lot of the believer (3:3–4).

SOME REVIEW QUESTIONS

1. What are two ways the work of God is hindered (see 2:14–16, 18)?
2. Did Paul think the Christian life is a bed of roses (3:3–4)?
3. How does believers' growth or lack of it affect your pastor (see 3:7–8)?
4. Will there ever be a time in this life when a Christian will not have some deficiencies in his or her life?
5. Think specifically about some shortcomings you should be working on.

8

PLEASING GOD

4:1–12

SECTION 4: INSTRUCTIONS AND EXHORTATIONS, 4:1–5:28

The first part of this letter was more personal, whereas this section emphasizes instructions and exhortations. Paul has already rather incidentally mentioned the deficiencies in the lives of the Thessalonians, and now he exhorts them to remedy these shortcomings. The section is marked off by the first two words, "finally then," which is an expression indicating the beginning of a new subject.

EXHORTATION TO ABOUND IN A LIFE THAT PLEASES GOD, 4:1–2

Before dealing with the specific things in which the believers needed attention, Paul opens this section with a general word of exhortation (vv. 1–2). He addresses the believers by the endearing term "brethren." Then he asks them to abound in the things they knew and were practicing. The verb "ask" (NIV) is *erotao*, which is generally used between those who are equal in rank, and this again shows Paul's esteem for these people. It is the only word for "ask" used by the Lord Jesus in His prayers to God (cf. John 14:16; 16:26; 17:9, 15, 20). This and 1 Thessalonians 5:12; 2 Thessalonians 2:1; and Philippians 4:3 are the only occurrences of the word in Paul's letters, and it is interesting to notice that they all occur in letters to Macedonian churches, as if to indicate that he held them in special esteem.

Paul also exhorts them, but not with any superior air, as the word "exhort" might imply, for his exhortation is "in the Lord." He reminds them that they had been told how they ought to walk and please God. "Ought" (NIV) denotes "moral necessity, lying in the relationship presupposed" (Findlay, *The Epistles of Paul the Apostle to the Thessalonians*, 81; cf. 2 Thess. 3:7; Rom. 1:28; etc.). Pleasing God is not a matter of choice for the Christian; it is a necessity that grows out of his relationship to Christ. Furthermore, pleasing God (cf. 1 Thess. 2:4; Rom. 2:29; 8:8; 1 Cor. 4:5; 7:32ff.; Gal. 1:10; 2 Tim. 2:4; Heb. 11:5–6) is something we will never complete in this life, for we must continually be abounding in it. The Christian life should be marked by constant growth. The phrase "just as you actually do walk" is omitted in some translations, but having good manuscript support and being a phrase Paul typically uses argue for its inclusion in the text.

Paul reminds his readers of the commandments he has given them. The word translated "commandments" is not a common one in the New Testament and signifies instruction given by a superior to a subordinate. It is often used of military orders. But these were no arbitrary commands of the apostle; they were given through the Lord Jesus, which is why he can exhort the believers to abound in them.

EXHORTATION TO BE SANCTIFIED, 4:3a

After this word of introduction, Paul deals with the first specific lack in the lives of the Thessalonians. It should be remembered that pagan life in those days was characterized by general sexual laxity. Ritual fornication played a large part in the heathen religious worship rites, and moral looseness was common among people on all levels of society. Since this was the environment in which the Thessalonians had been reared, it is easy to see why they did not have strong convictions and high standards for these areas of life. Nevertheless, Christianity does not take its standards from the society in which it is planted; it receives them from God Himself. Therefore, Paul deals with this matter of fornication in no uncertain terms.

He begins by putting the whole subject on the highest plane —"this is the will of God, your sanctification" (v. 3a). To "sanctify" means to set apart for God—the word is related to the words for holy and saints. There are three aspects to sanctification: (1) Positional sanctification, meaning that every believer has been sanctified in Christ, set apart to God the moment he or she believes (1 Cor. 6:11; Heb. 10:10). This is why the New Testament can call all believers, regardless of their spiritual condition, "saints" (1 Cor. 1:2) or "holy ones" (cf. 3:13 NIV). "Thus sainthood, or sanctification, is not an attainment, it is the state into which God, in grace, calls sinful men, and in which they begin their course as Christians" (Hogg and Vine, *The Epistles of Paul the Apostle to the Thessalonians,* 114) (2) Progressive sanctification. Sanctification is also used in the Scriptures of the goal of life that every believer should be pursuing (Heb. 12:14), and that involves separation from evil things and (in this passage) from fornication in particular. This progressive aspect is the use of sanctification here. (3) Ultimate sanctification. When we arrive in heaven, then and only then will we be completely set apart to God in holiness (3:13; Eph. 5:27).

Christians often ask, even debate, what the will of God is or how to know it in a particular circumstance or problem. Scripture specifically tells us several things that are undebatably the will of God. They are: (1) sanctification, or holiness, in sexual purity (1 Thess. 4:3), (2) redeeming the time we are given (Eph. 5:15–17); (3) doing our work as unto the Lord (Eph. 6:6); (4) praying without ceasing and thankfully (1 Thess. 5:17–18); and (5) obeying the various governments under which we live (1 Pet. 2:13–15). If one is grounded in these basic, unalterable, nonnegotiable and clear areas of obeying the will of God, discovery of God's will in particular circumstances will be much easier.

EXHORTATION TO SEXUAL PURITY, 4:3–8

THE MEANING OF IMMORALITY, 4:3b

The word includes not only adultery and fornication but also all kinds of illicit or natural sexual indulgence. Verse 3 states the requirement negatively ("from sexual immorality"), whereas verse 4 relates it positively.

THE MEANS OF EXPERIENCING SEXUAL PURITY: PROPERLY "POSSESSING ONE'S VESSEL," 4:4

Debate exists over the meaning of "vessel." Some think it means "body" and that Paul is saying that the believer is to gain the mastery over his body in order to keep himself pure in matters of sex. If this be the meaning, the idea is similar to that of 1 Corinthians 9:24–27, and the use of "vessel" is somewhat parallel to 2 Corinthians 4:7. Others think the word "vessel" means "wife," as in 1 Peter 3:7, and that the verb "possess" indicates proper courtship and contracting of marriage. In this case, Paul is expressing an idea similar to that in 2 Corinthians 7:2, and verse 4 here describes the honorable entry into matrimony, while verse 5 concerns the proper maintenance of that estate.

In either case—that is, whether Paul is referring to the chastity of one's own body or the relation with one's own wife—he declares that it should not be in lust as is the case with the Gentiles. In a marriage dominated by lust, there can be no honor or sanctity in the union. The word lust "signifies not, like [the English] 'passion,' a violent feeling, but an overmastering feeling, in which the man is borne along by evil as though its passive instrument" (Findlay, *The Epistles of Paul the Apostle to the Thessalonians*, 86). This was true of the Gentile neighbors of the Thessalonian believers, and it was true because they "[knew] not God," i.e., they had rejected the light that God had given them (see Rom. 1:21, 28).

THE CONSEQUENCES OF IMMORALITY, 4:5–8

Immorality dishonors one's own body (v. 5). Lust, rather than love, rules. It defrauds others (v. 6). This verse is probably to be understood as the result of obedience to the injunctions of verses 3 and 4. If fornication is abstained from, no man will transgress or, literally, go beyond his brother. To "transgress" means "to overreach," whereas "defraud" has the idea of taking advantage and implies avarice and covetousness. A sexual sin is a fraud against a brother, because it takes what is rightly his. Paul uses "brother" here not in the restricted sense of a brother in Christ but in the general sense of a brother man. There is no other instance in Paul's writings of this use of "brother." Paul reminds his readers that unbecoming conduct will not go unpunished, for "the Lord is the avenger of all such" (KJV).

Another reason for heeding the exhortation of verses 3 through 6 is stated in verses 7 and 8. The Christian should maintain purity of life not only from fear that God will judge (v. 6b) but also because of the grandeur of his calling in Christ to holiness. Two different prepositions are used in verse 7. God has "not called us unto ("with a view to") uncleanness" (KJV). The idea is purpose. Rather, He has called us in holiness. Sanctification as used in this passage, then, is not the ultimate aim, nor the gradual attainment of the Christian life, but it is the ruling condition and atmosphere in which the believer lives. Since this is so, therefore (v. 8 is a conclusion), to despise this truth is to despise God. To treat lightly the commands of the apostle with regard to sexual purity (v. 2) is to attempt to treat lightly the One whose standards cannot be disregarded. Thus, behind the commandments of the missionaries lay the immutable laws of God Himself. And it is this God who has made victory possible for the believer by giving the Holy Spirit.

"Gives" is a present tense participle, not indicating that God repeatedly gives the Holy Spirit but that He is the giver of the Spirit. Note the similar construction used in 1:10 to describe Jesus as the deliverer from the coming wrath. The Spirit is given at the time of salvation (Rom. 8:9), and He continues to be the available inner power for victory (cf. 1 Cor. 6:19). "The way to escape the Avenger is to fly to the Giver and accept and cherish His gift" (Plummer, *A Commentary on St. Paul's First Epistle to the Thessalonians*, 64).

EXHORTATION TO BROTHERLY LOVE, 4:9–10

Christianity should always be distinguished by purity and love. This latter is the next thing in which Paul asks the Thessalonians to abound.

THE EXPLANATION OF LOVE, 4:9

Paul speaks in these verses not of love in general but of brotherly love *(philadelphia)*. This means the love that particularly binds together the children of one father. Love is the seeking of the highest good for the one loved, and the highest good is the glory or manifestation of God. Therefore, brotherly love is that special desire to seek the glory of God in the lives of other members of the household of faith. This is something Paul says he need not write about, for God Himself teaches it (see John 13:34).

THE EXTENT OF LOVE, 4:10

This kind of love is to extend to "all the brethren" (4:10). The extent of love should be limited only by the opportunities afforded to express it.

THE EXPRESSION OF LOVE, 4:10

Paul probably has in the back of his mind here the way the Thessalonians expressed their love for their brethren by providing hospitality. This is one of the principal means of showing love (cf. Rom. 12:13; 1 Tim. 3:2; Titus 1:8; Heb. 13:1–2; 1 Pet. 4:9), and since Thessalonica was the commercial center of Macedonia, the believers there had undoubtedly many occasions to play host to Christians from other places.

THE EXPANSION OF LOVE, 4:10

Paul urges the increase of such love, for in brotherly love there is always room for growth. "Excel" in verse 10 is the same word as in verse 1.

EXHORTATION TO HAVE CORRECT AMBITIONS, 4:11–12

Following the admonition concerning love, Paul now urges his readers to have certain proper ambitions. The word for "be ambitious" is used elsewhere only in Romans 15:20 (to preach the Gospel where Christ was not known) and in 2 Corinthians 5:9 (to be pleasing to God). First, he exhorts them to be ambitious to be distinguished in being "quiet." Quiet is the opposite of restlessness (as Luke 14:4; 23:56; Acts 11:18). It means tranquility of mind, and this comes only when one's whole desire is to let Christ be magnified in his life. When selfish ambitions are the governing principles of life, there can only be unrest. But when Christ completely controls, there will be rest and the experience of this admonition to be ambitious to have no ambition of one's own.

Such an attitude (ambition) will also involve two things: tending to one's own affairs (2 Thess. 3:11–12) and working with one's own hands (2 Thess. 3:10). There is evidence that some of these believers were restless because they believed that there was no need to work, since the Lord would come very soon. Therefore, they may have been sponging off the other Christians in the church. Paul undoubtedly had these people in mind when giving these injunctions. The great purpose of a dedicated life that tends to its own business is to have an honest testimony toward the unsaved world.

"Properly" means "becomingly" or "decently," and the thought is related in this verse to those who are outside the Christian faith. Here Paul is urging the Thessalonians so to live that the unbelievers may see in their lives the difference between order and confusion, idleness and diligence, sponging and self-supporting. Such a life will be independent of the help of others, and this is the meaning of the last phrase in verse 12. Maintain an honorable independence and thus maintain a decent testimony to unbelievers.

9
THE RAPTURE

4:13–18

As has been suggested, the cause of restlessness among some of the Thessalonian Christians was the belief that, since the Lord's coming was imminent, there was no point in working any longer. Too, the seeming delay in the Lord's return made them concerned about when they might expect relief from the persecutions they were experiencing. Also, that delay caused them to wonder about the destiny of those who died before the Lord's coming. It is clear that Paul had taught much about this subject while he was in the city (2 Thess. 2:5), but the main point of his teaching had evidently concerned the coming of Christ and not the resurrection. In the meantime, perhaps some of the believers had died, and the question arose, "Has their premature death caused them to lose all hope of sharing in the glorious reign of Christ?"

The fact that this question did arise points to the early date of the epistle, for only in the early years of the church, when but a few had had time to die, could it have caused such great anxiety. That agitation had arisen over this matter was probably reported to Paul by Timothy on his return from Thessalonica. Paul's answer to the problem is a reassuring affirmation that the

dead will be raised and will therefore share in the kingdom, and
that the living at Christ's return would be changed and taken
into His presence.

WE HAVE A PREVIEW, 4:13–14

The certainty of the Christian's resurrection is based on the
fact of Christ's resurrection. The formula "I would not have you
to be uninformed" is found frequently in Paul's writings when he
wishes to explain some new point (cf. Rom. 1:13; 11:25; 1 Cor.
10:1; 12:1; 2 Cor. 1:8). The subject here is "those who are
asleep." The present participle is used (signifying continuousness) and can mean either "those that are lying asleep" or
"those who fall asleep from time to time." The verb "to sleep"
is used of natural sleep (Matt. 28:13; Acts 12:6; etc.); of spiritual laziness and indifference (Rom. 13:11; Eph. 5:14; 1 Thess.
5:6); and of physical death, but only the death of a Christian (as
here and 1 Cor. 15:51; 2 Pet. 3:4; etc.). The word is particularly
suggestive when used in the latter sense.

> The object of the metaphor is to suggest that as the sleeper does
> not cease to exist while his body sleeps, so the dead person contin-
> ues to exist despite his absence from the region in which those
> who remain can communicate with him, and that, as sleep is
> known to be temporary, so the death of the body will be found to
> be [temporary]. Sleep has its waking, death will have its resurrec-
> tion. (Hogg and Vine, *The Epistles of Paul the Apostle to the
> Thessalonians*, 128)

Because of this, any sorrow the Christian may have over the
loss of a loved one (and it is comforting to remember that our
Lord wept when His friend Lazarus died [John 11:33–35]) is un-
like the hopeless despair that the heathen can only have.

Paul is not saying that Christians may not sorrow but that
they should not sorrow to the same degree as the pagans, for the
meaning not to sorrow at all would strain the "as." He is saying
that Christians are not to be like the heathen, because Christians do not sorrow as they do. For the pagan, the loss is an
unsustainable deprivation. For the Christian, the loss and resul-

tant grief are temporary. He does not deny that we may grieve over loss (cf. Phil. 2:27), but believers must not have the same kind of sorrow that characterizes unbelievers. "Against this deep sorrow of the world, the word *sleep,* four times applied in this context to the Christian's death, is an abiding protest" (Findlay, *The Epistles of Paul the Apostle to the Thessalonians,* 96).

The teaching of soul sleep (i.e., that the soul sleeps between death and resurrection) has been held sporadically in the history of the church. The idea is based on the fact that soul and body are a unity; therefore, if the body is said to sleep, so also must the soul, and the concept of sleep includes a cessation of consciousness, which would apply to the soul as well as the body at death. However, continued consciousness after death is an integral part of the Lord's account of the rich man and Lazarus (Luke 16:19–31). Paul's clear teaching that at death the believer is present with the Lord contradicts the idea of soul sleep (2 Cor. 5:8; Phil. 1:23). John saw the souls of martyrs in heaven conversing with the Lord after their deaths (Rev. 6:9–10).

This certainty is based on the preview seen in the resurrection of Christ. The "if" clause is a first-class condition and assumes the fact. Therefore it may be translated "since we believe." The condition being true, the result is also true—that is, God will bring with Christ into His kingdom those who have fallen asleep through Jesus. The last phrase, "in Jesus" (better "through Jesus"), is related to the fact that death has been changed to sleep through the work of Jesus. By sharp contrast, the hopelessness of the pagans when facing death is seen in the following quotation from a letter of the second century:

> Eirene to Taormophris and Philon, good cheer! I was as much grieved and shed as many tears over Eumoiros as I shed for Didymas, and I did everything that was fitting, and so did my whole family. But still there is nothing one can do in the face of such trouble. So I leave you to comfort yourselves. Good-bye." (Deissman, *New Light on the New Testament,* 76).

"For [Christians] to give way to their grief would be to act like the pagan world," (Hiebert, *The Thessalonian Epistles,* 189).

We Have a Promise, 4:15

Next comes the positive declaration that the Christian dead will actually be raised first and will therefore undoubtedly have a share in the kingdom. The statement is made as authoritative as possible by stating that it is the word of the Lord. There are two possible explanations of how Paul knew this was a word from the Lord. It could be an otherwise unrecorded saying of Christ (as is Acts 20:35), or it may have come to Paul by direct revelation (cf. Acts 16:6; 18:9–10). In any case, the Thessalonians need not be worried; in reality the dead will have a foremost place, for the living shall "in no wise" (RV) (emphatic negative) precede those who are asleep at the Lord's return.

Notice that Paul included himself among that living group and evidently expected to live until the return of Christ (cf. Phil. 4:5 and Titus 2:13, written later in his life). One of the wonderful things about the hope of His coming is that it burns brightly in the hearts of each generation of Christians, regardless of how long His return is delayed.

We Have a Picture, 4:16–18

Paul now fills in the details of the picture of what will happen when the Lord returns.

A Return, 4:16

Christ "Himself" will return. The word "Himself" is in the emphatic position in the sentence and emphasizes that no intermediary, but the Lord Himself, will usher in this great event. Because it will be He Himself who comes, the attendant circumstances will display all the grandeur due His personal presence. There will be a shout. It is a word of command used in classical Greek for the shout with which an officer gives the order to his troops or his crew. There is in the word a ring of authority and a note of urgency. It is not said who utters the shout, whether it is the Lord or an archangel. However, the voice of an archangel will be heard.

Michael is the only archangel mentioned in the Bible (Jude 9), but it is not impossible that there are other archangels (notice the absence of the definite article here—*an* archangel, not *the* archangel). Notice also Daniel 10:13, which designates Michael as "one of the chief princes." Though Gabriel is mentioned as a high-ranking angel (Dan. 8:16; 9:21; Luke 1:19, 26), he is not specifically designated as an archangel. The Jews listed seven chief angels altogether. The trumpet of God will also sound when He comes. This is also referred to twice in 1 Corinthians 15:52.

A RESURRECTION, 4:16

Again the priority of the dead is mentioned, for they shall be raised first. It is not that they shall be raised before the rest of the dead but before those who are alive at the Lord's coming are changed. "Dead in Christ" is a synonymous description of those who "sleep in Jesus" (KJV).

The phrase "in Christ" seems to restrict the group raised to believers of this age (since the Day of Pentecost) and not believers of all time. If this is so, then one would assume that Old Testament believers will be raised at the second coming of Christ.

A RAPTURE, 4:17

Next in order ("then," *epeita,* implies order of events and not necessarily any lengthy interval between) there will be the change in the living. We shall be "caught up." The word means "seize" or "snatch," and the Latin translation of this verb uses the word from which we get "rapture" in English. Thus the translation of living believers is called the rapture of the church. Rapture means the act of conveying a person from one place to another and thus is properly used of this transport of the living to heaven. Paul used it of his own experience of being caught up to the third heaven (2 Cor. 12:2, 4; cf. also Acts 8:39 and Rev. 12:5). The word also includes the idea of seizing hastily (Acts 23:10). It seems clear from these other occurrences of the word that Paul had in mind being taken to another location, i.e., heaven, and not just into midair to turn around suddenly and return to the earth (as posttribulationism teaches).

He also implies in this idea of rapture the necessary change in mortal bodies in order to fit them for immortal existence in heaven. This is stated in greater detail in 1 Corinthians 15:50–53. And although the method of this change is never revealed, it is clear that Paul believed it is possible to have a metamorphosis without the dissolution caused by death.

A REUNION, 4:17

The reunion is actually twofold. It is first of all with loved ones who have died, for we shall be caught up together *with* them. Second, it is a meeting with the Lord in the air (with a view to proceeding on into heaven, not returning to the earth immediately, as in the posttribulation scenario). "The natural consequence of this blissful meeting with the Lord is that there will be no subsequent parting" (Plummer, *A Commentary on St. Paul's First Epistle to the Thessalonians*, 77). After His return there will be uninterrupted union and communion with our Lord.

A REASSURANCE, 4:18

As a result of what has been stated, there should be no sorrowing but rather comfort concerning those who have died. Notice how Paul sticks to the subject—the dead in Christ. He says nothing in this passage about the resurrection of the wicked, the intermediate state, judgment, means of translation, or reign with Christ. In this passage, our hope is centered on the assurance of the resurrection of the dead in Christ, the change in the living, and the eternal union with our Lord. Repeating these truths will bring assurance to the heart.

Erich Sauer throws light on some additional facets of the Rapture that are often overlooked:

[At the Rapture] for the first time the church of all times and all lands will be with one another. Thus the completed church will exist for the first time, but not on earth but in the air (1 Thess.

4:17). Till then there exist only churches (in the plural, Rev. 22:16), and the church of a *generation* living at any one time on earth. . . . *Triumph!* For the air is the very base of operations of the Enemy. It is from the air that the world is at present ruled by demon powers. . . . But now exactly in the region of his power, at the very headquarters of the conquered foe, there takes place the meeting of the Conqueror, and His victorious hosts. The triumph cannot be greater; a more glorious festival of victory cannot be. Christ has conquered completely. His church had overcome absolutely. Therefore the crowning of the persecuted takes place at the headquarters of their defeated Persecutor (Sauer, *The Triumph of the Crucified,* 105–6).

10

THE DAY OF THE LORD

5:1–11

INSTRUCTION AND EXHORTATIONS CONCERNING THE DAY OF THE LORD, 5:1–11

A DEFINITION OF THE DAY OF THE LORD

It is a time of God's special intervention in the affairs of human history. The use of the phrase in the Bible includes three facets of the Day of the Lord: (1) Historical—God's intervention in the affairs of Israel and pagan nations (Ezek. 30:3; Zeph. 1:14–18), (2) Illustrative—a historical event that illustrates some future aspect of the Day (Joel 2:1–11), and (3) Future—which includes the coming Tribulation years (Isa. 2:12–19; 4:1), the second coming of Christ (Joel 2:30–32), and the Millennium (Isa. 4:2; 12), sometimes focusing on one or another of these future events.

THE RELATION OF THE DAY OF THE LORD TO THE RAPTURE OF THE CHURCH, 5:1

The opening phrase of verse 5:1 (two words in the Greek, translated "but" or "now") indicates that the Day of the Lord does not include the Rapture. That opening phrase, *peri de,* Paul uses regularly in his letters to introduce a new subject (see 1 Cor. 7:1, 25; 8:1; 12:1; 16:1, 12; 1 Thess. 4:9; 5:1). Therefore, Paul is indicating that the "Day of the Lord" is a new subject from the Rapture, which he has described in the preceding paragraph. This conclusion is reinforced by the fact that Paul elsewhere calls the Rapture a mystery (1 Cor. 15:51), which is something not revealed in the Old Testament but revealed in the New Testament. The Rapture is not revealed in the Old Testament, whereas the Day of the Lord is. The expression "day of the Lord" occurs 20 times; "last days," 14 times; "that day," 100 times. Obviously the Day of the Lord was well known from the Old Testament and was included in Paul's teaching about the future. Since the Rapture is not a part of the Day of the Lord, then it must occur before the beginning of the Day, i.e., before the Tribulation begins. Thus the Rapture cannot be within the Tribulation (midtribulationism) or at the end with the Second Coming (posttribulationism).

To summarize, Paul's use of *peri de* and his contrast between the Rapture unrevealed in the Old Testament and the Day of the Lord often taught in the Old Testament strongly support a pretribulation rapture of the church.

THE BEGINNING OF THE DAY OF THE LORD, 5:2–3

A second matter in relation to the return of Christ comes up for discussion. Not only were the believers concerned about the fate of loved ones who died before the return, but, like so many others, they wanted to know something about *when* the event would occur. The disciples also had asked when (Mark 13:3–4), and the Lord had told them that He could not give them any new light on the question (Acts 1:7). Paul, too, appeals to what they already know and asks them to wait patiently and work hard in the meantime.

We need not think that the question was prompted by idle curiosity. If the time of the appearing is unknown, it is natural to be apprehensive about whether anyone now alive will live to see it. Paul tries to show his readers that certain things about the coming of the Lord are more important than whether they would be alive when it occurs.

Although the future Day of the Lord will include the Tribulation, Second Coming, and the Millennium, in this passage Paul is not discussing the entire Day of the Lord but only its coming, its beginning. This is important, for it explains why he deals only with the judgment aspect of that day. Also, this is something that was known to them from both the Old Testament and Paul's own teaching (cf. 2 Thess. 2:1–4).

Remember that the first words of verse 1 indicate a contrast. This shows that the subject preceding, i.e., the rapture of the living and the resurrection of the dead in Christ, was not included in Old Testament revelation or in Paul's teaching while with them. The very fact that these Christians did not know about the Rapture and resurrection of believers accounts for their perplexity about it.

But of the Day of the Lord they should have known perfectly well. They became confused about it later (as seen from 2 Thess. 2), but it could not be blamed on the fact that they could not know, either from the Old Testament or from a careful listening to Paul's teaching. In particular, they knew about the times (the duration) and the seasons (the characteristics) of the Day of the Lord, especially as they related to the beginning of that Day. It would be as a thief in the night. "The unexpectedness of the coming of the thief, and the unpreparedness of those to whom he comes, are the essential elements in this figure" (Hogg and Vine, *The Epistles of Paul the Apostle to the Thessalonians*, 154). The same simile is used by Christ in Matthew 24:43 and Revelation 3:3.

The beginning of the Day of the Lord will come with delusion and destruction. It will delude because men will be saying (the verb is in the continuous present tense), "Peace and safety," when the Day overtakes them. At the very moment the world feels secure (this is the meaning of the rather rare word translated "safety," cf. Luke 1:4; Acts 5:23, for its only other occurrences), and people are assuring themselves and each other that all is well, sudden destruction will come on them.

Destruction is not annihilation but "utter and hopeless *ruin,* the loss of all that gives worth to existence" (Milligan, *St Paul's Epistles to the Thessalonians*, 65). This is compared with birth pangs, a familiar simile in the Scriptures (Isa. 13:6–8; 37:3; Hos. 13:13; Mic. 4:9; Mark 13:8), and the comparison involves inevitable certainty, suddenness, and intense pain. The certainty is particularly emphasized in this passage by the last clause, "they shall not escape" (KJV). There are several similarities of language in this verse to Luke 21:34, a fact that is not surprising in light of the friendship between Paul and Luke. Nowhere in Revelation 4 to 19, chapters that describe the coming Tribulation period, is there any time of "peace and safety" except at the very beginning under the first seal judgment (for peace is not removed from the earth until the second seal judgment (Rev. 6:1–2 compared with v. 4).

THE EXHORTATIONS TO BELIEVERS IN LIGHT OF THE COMING OF THE DAY OF THE LORD, 5:4–11

Truth is practical, and the doctrine of the Day of the Lord and particularly its sudden coming is intensely so.

REMEMBER YOU ARE ALL SONS OF LIGHT, 5:4–5

This is true because we belong to Christ, who is Light. The coming of the Day of the Lord will be a great divider between children of light and children of darkness. Thus it behooves one to examine himself and be sure to which group he belongs. With a strong "but you," Paul expresses his confidence that the Thessalonians are children of light. Negatively, they are not children of darkness (v. 4), and positively they are children of the day (v. 5). "Darkness" describes the condition of unbelievers who live in the sphere and condition of darkness, blinded to the light of the Gospel. There exists no twilight between light and darkness— every person is either in darkness or, through faith in Christ, in light. The reference to day in verse 5 is to the Day of the Lord mentioned earlier in verse 2, and Paul assures his readers (and us) that we will not be a part of that day of darkness. Similarly, Joel calls the Day of the Lord a day of darkness, gloominess, cloudiness, and thick darkness (Joel 2:2). The only way that believers, who are not children of darkness, will not be overtaken by that day of darkness is that we will have been taken up to heaven in the pretribulation Rapture described in 4:13–18.

Don't be Asleep, Watch, Be Sober, 5:6–8

Watching involves alertness. In other passages it is linked with prayer (Mark 13:33–34; Col. 4:2). It is the opposite of indifference, which carries the idea of "sleep" in verse 6. This is a different word for sleep from that used in 4:13 and following and is regularly used of moral indifference and lack of vigilance (cf. Mark 13:36; Eph. 5:14). Some think this refers to unbelievers who are dead in sin, this being the meaning of "sleep" here. Thus they are being called to salvation. Others understand that this exhortation not to be asleep relates to indifferent believers. Can believers be described as "asleep," that is, indifferent to spiritual things? Certainly, and that seems to be the group Paul is warning here, since he contrasts them with "others," that is, unbelievers. Regrettably, believers can live like unsaved people (1 Cor. 3:3).

Watching involves being alert and is connected with prayer in Mark 13:34–37 and Colossians 4:2. Sobriety excludes actual drunkenness (Luke 12:45; though there is no implication that these people were given to that) and self-indulgence (1 Tim. 3:2; Titus 2:2). The word is used outside the New Testament for wineless offerings, and it emphasizes the need for stability, balance, and complete control of one's life in view of the Lord's return. Be spiritual (not carnal), be alert, and be sober are Paul's exhortations.

These exhortations of verse 6 are reinforced in verse 7 by reminding the readers that those who are of the night do the very opposite. They sleep and are drunk. This is to be understood in its natural sense and as a statement of the facts of life. But the natural is used in an analogy with the spiritual. As sleep is natural in the night, so indifference to God is natural for the believer who lives like an unsaved man. As drunkenness is natural at night, so instability is natural to the carnal Christian. But the redeemed are not of the night; therefore, let us be alert and be sober.

The Christian's sobriety evidently brought to Paul's mind the picture of a soldier on duty, and therefore he mentions the believer's armor (v. 8; cf. Rom. 13:12; Eph. 6:11–17). The tenses in the Greek are revealing. "Be sober" is present tense, indicating that this should be the continual attitude of the Christian, whereas "putting on" (KJV) is aorist, which expresses an event. The tense says, "Put your armor on and leave it on." The breastplate, which covered the soldier's body from neck to waist, consists of faith and love, and the helmet is the hope of salvation. Here once again we see the triad of Christian graces—faith, hope, and love. Although the details of the particular pieces of armor differ in the different passages where the figure is used, in no passage is a piece covering the back mentioned, for the Christian once engaged in the fight should not turn in flight.

BE ENCOURAGED, 5:9–11

The hope of salvation, which is the helmet mentioned in the previous verse, means the full realization and experience of our salvation in the future. The assurance of this hope's being fulfilled is the fact that God has appointed us not to wrath but to salvation. "Appointed" (KJV) is not as strong as "predestined" (as in Rom. 8:29), but it does mean that God did not place us in wrath but put us into salvation. The wrath is the anguish and tribulation associated with the beginning of the Day of the Lord (v. 3), and it is from this that the believer has been delivered by the One who "delivers us from the wrath to come" (1:10 NKJV). Instead, we are to obtain salvation, and this has been effected through the Lord Jesus Christ and based on His death (v. 10). His death also effected our union with Him, which in turn guarantees that whether we are awake (alive on earth at the Rapture) or asleep (dead at that time as far the body is concerned), we will live with Him. This is the source of comfort and edification (v. 11; cf. 4:18).

The fact that in verse 10 is the only mention of the death of

Christ in this Paul's earliest letter does not mean that Paul was still developing his theology. He had been saved for nearly a score of years and had been actively in the Lord's work for almost a decade before this letter was written. The subject matter of the letter concerns other topics, and in reality the very fact that he mentions the death of Christ at all in the midst of discussions of other subjects shows how firmly it was a part of his overall doctrine. It is also interesting to notice the brief mention here of the doctrine of union with Christ, which Paul expounds elaborately in other epistles. Since this is not the subject here, either, it shows that this major doctrine was already firmly fixed in Paul's mind and theology.

11
VARIOUS RESPONSIBILITIES IN THE CHURCH

5:12–24

INSTRUCTIONS FOR THOSE WHO ARE LED BY LEADERS IN THE CHURCH, 5:12–13

In these two verses Paul describes what leaders should do and the proper response to their leadership by those who are being led. He admonishes the congregation to "appreciate" and "esteem" their leaders and be at peace with each other. Two factors made these admonitions especially important for the Thessalonian church. First, there was the problem caused by those who had stopped working because of their belief in the nearness of the Second Coming. Undoubtedly, the leaders had rebuked them, and the rebuke had not been well received. Therefore, Paul enjoins them to listen to the rulers of the church. Second, all the members of this church were new Christians, and most had been converted about the same time. Some, however, had become officers in the church. It must have been difficult for some to take instruction from those whom they had known all their lives and who had been saved about the same time.

While it is true that in the church all have equal spiritual privileges and blessings, it is not true that all have equal offices or responsibilities, for there are differences of gifts, and among these gifts is the gift of government, which not every believer has (1 Cor. 12:28). If there are those who govern, there are those who are governed. To this latter group Paul says three things: know and appreciate the leaders, esteem them very highly, and be at peace. To know in the fullest sense means to know the function and responsibilities of leaders and to appreciate them. To esteem (v. 13) is to think highly of their leaders. "Esteem" is followed by the same doubly compounded word as in 3:10 and means to esteem the leaders exceedingly highly in love because of their ministry. To be at peace means no schism, and this injunction is broadened to include all.

In these two verses, leaders are described in the plural, which indicates there were several, not just one, in the congregation and argues for a plurality of elders (or leaders, whatever be their label) in a local congregation.

Instructions for Those Who Lead, 5:12–13

In these verses, Paul describes the duties of the leaders. He focuses on three things: they labor, they preside, and they admonish the people. It is clear that these are the duties of the same persons because of the single article before the three participles that describe their work. It is not too early in the history of the church to have had officers, for Paul appointed elders as early as the return leg of his first missionary journey (Acts 14:23). In general, these elders were to labor (this is the same word that appears in noun form in 1 Thess. 1:3). It means the kind of work that causes one to grow weary in the doing of it—to toil with effort is the idea. It is a favorite word of Paul's, used frequently to describe the arduous character of his own ministry (cf. 1 Cor. 15:10; Gal. 4:11; Phil. 2:16; Col. 1:29; 1 Tim. 4:10).

In particular, the leaders were over the people; that is, they "presided over" the affairs of the church. This verb for *preside* is found elsewhere in the New Testament in Romans 12:8; 1 Timothy 3:4–5, 12; 5:17; and Titus 3:8. To preside is not to dictate, and yet it is to be in a position of leadership that includes both direction and a certain amount of control. Too, these officers were to admonish the people (KJV). The word means literally "to put in mind" and "has apparently always a sense of *blame* attached to it" (Milligan, *St Paul's Epistles to the Thessalonians*, 72). That is why this same word is translated "warn" in verse 14 (KJV).

It is because of the discharge of the responsibilities of leaders that they are to be highly thought of (v. 13). Leaders' reputations should result primarily from the quality of their work rather than for other reasons.

INSTRUCTIONS FOR THE ENTIRE GROUP, 5:14–15

The words of verse 14 are not specifically addressed to the leaders and show that certain duties are the responsibility of the entire congregation. However, because of what has just been said, they have some special reference to the officers, if only that they are to take the lead in carrying them out. There are twelve specific things to be done.

WARN THE UNRULY, 5:14a

For the meaning of "warn" (KJV), see the previous discussion on "admonish." The word "unruly" is a military term signifying the soldier who does not keep in proper rank. Thus it came to mean anything out of order and may in this present passage have particular reference to idleness and neglect of responsibilities.

ENCOURAGE THE FAINTHEARTED, 5:14b

The word literally means "little-souled." Perhaps the reference in this context is to those who were discouraged because some of their loved ones had died before the appearing of the Lord, and they needed encouragement. However, it can refer to all who are discouraged for whatever reason.

HELP THE WEAK, 5:14c

Although "weak" can refer to physical ailments (see Phil. 2:26) or financial distress (Acts 20:35), here the word likely refers to those who were weak in their spiritual lives. Symptoms of spiritual weakness could be instability, inability to face persecution, or yielding to the attacks of Satan, all of which may have been present in the Thessalonian church. "These, and all such as these, are to be the peculiar objects of the shepherd's care, since, more than the rest, they need the sympathy and help of those who are of maturer Christian experience" (Hogg and Vine, *The Epistles of Paul the Apostle to the Thessalonians*, 183).

Be Long-suffering Toward All, 5:14d

"Be longsuffering" ("patient") literally means "be long-tempered" and is the exact opposite of "be short-tempered." This is to be the characteristic of the Christian in relation to all people.

Do Not Render Evil for Evil, 5:15a

This prohibition of retaliation is found also in Romans 12:17 and 1 Peter 3:9. It was particularly apropos in the case of the Thessalonian Christians, who were faced with persecution. It must have been difficult for some not to want to retaliate under those pressures. But Paul does not hesitate to put the matter plainly to them.

Follow That Which Is Good, 5:15b

The good is that which is especially helpful to others, the beneficial. This is to be the rule of life always and to all men.

Always Rejoice, 5:16

The command to rejoice always is somewhat of a wake-up call to suffering people. It must have struck the readers as something of a paradox, and yet Paul had learned the secret of true joy. It must not depend on circumstances, for in the world the Christian will have tribulation (John 16:33). The ground for lasting joy is found in eternal things: in the Lord (Phil. 3:1), in the Gospel (John 4:36: Acts 13:48), and in seeing fellow believers grow in the truth (3 John 4). Incidentally, this verse, not John 11:35 ("Jesus wept"), is the shortest verse in the Greek New Testament.

BE PRAYERFUL, 5:17

The Christian's joy puts him in the proper mood to pray without ceasing. Paul has already used "without ceasing" twice of his own prayerful remembrance of the Thessalonians (1:3; 2:13 KJV), and now he enjoins it on the believers. Outside the New Testament, the word is used of a hacking cough and aptly illustrates what Paul has in mind here about prayer. Just as a person with a hacking cough is not always audibly coughing, the tendency to cough, the tickle, is always there, so the Christian who prays without ceasing is not always praying audibly, and yet prayer is always the attitude of his heart and life.

BE THANKFUL, 5:18

This injunction concludes with the exhortation to be thankful in every circumstance (cf. Eph. 5:20; Phil. 4:6; Col. 3:17). The meaning is not that we are to be thankful *for* everything, but in the midst of any situation or circumstance we should find causes for thanksgiving in what God has done for us. Rejoicing, praying, thanking—this triad of precepts is without question the will of God for the believer.

DO NOT QUENCH THE WORK OF THE SPIRIT, 5:19

This concerns the work of the Holy Spirit in the individual and in the assembly, and condemns quenching, or extinguishing, His ministry. The word *quench* is used of putting out a fire (Mark 9:48; Heb. 11:34) and is used in connection with the Spirit (cf. Matt. 3:11; Acts 2:3). The tense is present, and since this is a command, it means "stop quenching the Spirit"; that is, stop doing something you are now doing, not merely beware of doing it at some future time. Evidently, the situation at Thessalonica was the opposite from that in Corinth, where Paul later had to warn the church against disorderliness in relation to the gifts of the Spirit. At Thessalonica, some were apparently frowning on any manifestation of the Spirit, whatever it was. This might be expected from the Macedonians, who were more advanced culturally than those who lived in the south of Greece. They would be more prone to want to stifle the exercise of the gifts of the Spirit.

Do Not Despise Prophesyings, 5:20

To despise is to treat with contempt or to reduce to nothing, and this is what some were apparently doing in relation to prophesying. At this period (before the New Testament books were completed) such prophesyings would have come as direct revelation from God. There are two aspects to prophesying: forthtelling (at Thessalonica this may have included the firm admonitions to the believers because of their idleness) and foretelling (and this may have involved messages concerning the Second Advent).

Examine, or Prove, Everything, 5:21–22

However, Paul does not advocate an uncritical acceptance of everything that claims to be of the Spirit. He requires the proving, or testing, of all things (v. 21; cf. 1 Cor. 12:3). That which is found to be good (the word means "genuine," in contrast to the counterfeit) should be heeded. "The chaff must be sifted out from the wheat" (Findlay, *The Epistles of Paul the Apostle to the Thessalonians*, 129). That which is evil should be shunned (v. 22). Every appearance or visible form of evil is to be avoided by the Christian. The word "form" could indicate every kind of evil whether visible or internal, but the uniform New Testament usage favors the idea "every visible form or outward show of evil" (Luke 3:22; 9:29; John 5:37). Different kinds of evil is a quasi-philosophical idea, but it is certainly true that evil appears in many different forms.

BE SANCTIFIED, 5:23–24

Finally, Paul exhorts his beloved readers to complete holiness (v. 23) on the basis of assured help from God (v. 24). "Wholly" (KJV) is found only here in the New Testament and is made up of two words, "complete" and "end." Thus both ideas of wholeness and completion are included. This is entire sanctification, and it is the work of God. It is further explained by the prayer that the whole spirit, soul, and body be preserved blameless. Some take this verse to prove the threefold nature of man (called trichotomy), but it is not best taken as a proof text for this. Paul is not analyzing man here (such an analysis would have to include "heart" and "mind") but is praying for complete sanctification in aim and in extent, and it is the faithfulness of God that assures the answer to the prayer.

12
CONCLUSION

5:25–28

In this conclusion to his letter, Paul makes a request and sends greetings, instructions, and a benediction. The request is a simple one for prayer for himself. Missionaries, pastors, Christian workers have problems and needs and therefore need the prayers of God's people, especially those who have been the recipients of their ministry. Similar requests are found in 2 Thessalonians 3:1ff.; Romans 15:30; Ephesians 6:19; and Colossians 4:3ff.

Greetings were given in the familiar form of the holy kiss (also in Rom. 16:16; 1 Cor. 16:20; 2 Cor. 13:12; 1 Pet. 5:14; and see Luke 7:45). Not too much is known of the custom except that it seemed to be the practice of the early church to greet one another on the Lord's Day with a kiss on the cheek, exchanged by members of both the same and opposite sex. Like other practices (e.g., the love feast), it became abused in due time and had to be restricted because of the poor testimony to the pagans.

The instruction to read the epistle is put in very strong language (v. 27). The word for "charge" (KJV) really means "to bind with an oath." He wanted to be certain that what he had said was read and heard by everyone in the group.

Finally, the epistle concludes with a prayer for grace for his readers, whom he loved so dearly in the Lord.

SECOND THESSALONIANS

INTRODUCTORY MATTERS

1. The place of writing: Corinth, where Paul, Silas, and Timothy were.
2. The date of writing: A.D. 51, shortly (probably two or three months) afer 1 Thessalonians.
3. The occasion of writing: Paul had received fresh news about the church that was both favorable (1:3–4) and unfavorable (3:6,11–12). Perhaps the bearer of 1 Thessalonians had brought back word to Paul concerning conditions in Thessalonica, or others had whose business had taken them to Corinth.
4. The purpose of the letter: to correct misunderstandings or misrepresentations of Paul's teaching about the future (2:2) and to correct the readers about certain practices in that church.

REVIEW QUESTIONS

1. Where was Paul when he wrote 2 Thessalonians?
2. How much time likely elapsed between the writing of 1 and 2 Thessalonians?
3. What was Paul's purpose in writing 2 Thessalonians?

OUTLINE OF SECOND THESSALONIANS

I. Introductory Matters
II. The Greeting (1:1–2)

SECTION 1: ENCOURAGEMENT IN PERSECUTION (1:3–12)

I. Encouragement from Paul's Gratitude for Their Growth
and Endurance (1:3–4)
   A. The Obligation Paul Felt to Be Thankful (1:3a)
   B. The Content of Paul's Thanksgiving (1:3b)
   C. The Consequences of Paul's Thanksgiving (1:4)
II. Encouragement from the Knowledge of Ultimate Relief
and Vindication (1:5–10)
   A. Encouragement from the Believers' Reaction to Perse-
   cution (1:5)
   B. Encouragement from the Second Coming of Christ
   (1:6–10)
      1. His retribution (1:6–9)
      2. His glorification (1:10)
III. Encouragement from Knowing Paul Was Praying for
Them (1:11–12)
   A. The Content of Paul's Prayer (1:11)
   B. The Purpose of Paul's Prayer (1:12)
   Addendum: The Rapture Debate and This Passage

SECTION 2: ENCOURAGEMENT FROM PROPHECY (2:1–17)

I. The Relation of the Day of the Lord to the Present (2:1–2)
   A. The Subject Matter of Paul's Teaching (2:1)
      1. The coming (2:1a)
      2. The gathering (2:1b)
   B. The Purpose of Paul's Teaching (2:2)
   C. The Bottom Line of Paul's Teaching (2:2b)
II. The Relation of the Day of the Lord to the Apostasy (2:3a)
   A. The Meaning of Apostasy
   B. The Time of the Apostasy

III. The Relation of the Day of the Lord to the Lawless One
(2:3b–5, 8–10)
  A. The Revelation of the Lawless One (2:2–3b)
    1. What it signals (2:3b)
    2. Who the Lawless One is (2:3b)
  B. The Religion of the Lawless One (2:4–5)
    1. In the first half of the Tribulation (Rev. 17)
    2. In the last half of the Tribulation (2:4)
  C. The Power of the Lawless One (2:9–10)
    1. The source of his power (2:9)
    2. The evidences of his power (2:10)
  D. The Punishment of the Lawless One (2:8)
    1. The means (2:8)
    2. The result (2:8)
IV. The Relation of the Day of the Lord to the Restrainer
(2:6–7)
  A. The Place of the Restrainer in the Order of Events
  B. The Work of the Restrainer
  C. The Identification of the Restrainer
  D. The Relation of the Restrainer to the Rapture of the
Church
 V. The Relation of the Day of the Lord to Unbelievers
(2:10–12)
  A. The Coming Delusion (2:11–12)
    1. Its origin (2:11a)
    2. Its purposes (2:11b)
  B. The Related Question (2:10, 12)
VI. The Relation of the Day of the Lord to the Believer
(2:13–17)
  A. The Believer's Position (2:13–14)
    1. Chosen (2:13)
    2. Called (2:14)
  B. The Believer's Practice (2:15–17)
    1. The exhortations (2:15)
    2. The prayer (2:16–17)

SECTION 3: ENCOURAGEMENT AND COMMANDS
CONCERNING VARIOUS PRACTICES (3:1–18)

  I. Paul's Request for Continued Prayer (3:1–2)
     A. Paul's Request for Prayer (3:1a)
     B. Paul's Petitions Stated (3:1b–2)
 II. Paul's Confidence (3:3–4)
     A. In the Faithfulness of the Lord (3:3)
     B. In the Obedience of the Thessalonians (3:4)
III. Paul's Prayer (3:5)
 IV. Commands Concerning the Unruly (3:6–10)
     A. The Penalty for the Unruly (3:6)
     B. The Pattern for the Unruly: Paul's Own Conduct (3:7–9)
     C. The Prescription for Unruliness (3:10)
  V. Commands Concerning Busybodies (3:11–12)
     A. The Description of Busybodies (3:11)
     B. The Cure for Busybodies (3:12)
 VI. Further Encouragement for Believers (3:13)
VII. Further Commands Concerning the Disobedient (3:14–15)
     A. Note Them (3:14)
     B. Disassociate from Them (3:14)
     C. Admonish Them (3:15)
VIII. Concluding Benediction and Greeting (3:16–18)
     A. Paul's Prayer for Peace (3:16)
     B. Paul's Personal Greeting (3:17)
     C. Paul's Prayer for Grace (3:18)

1
THE GREETING

1:1–2

The greeting in this epistle is longer than that in the first one. It begins in the customary manner, that is, with the name of the writer followed by that of the recipient. Again Silas and Timothy are linked with Paul, not because they were coauthors of the letter but because they had shared the ministry at Thessalonica. The church, too, is addressed in the same way as in the first letter —"the church of the Thessalonians"—a way that is different from the customary designations in the other Pauline Epistles. The only difference between the first verses of the two letters is the addition of the word "our" in this one, emphasizing God's fatherhood in relation to believers. This should have been especially comforting to a church that was suffering persecution to realize that, though suffering, her position was in God our Father and the Lord Jesus Christ, a place of protection and security.

The second verse pronounces grace and peace "from God our Father and the Lord Jesus Christ" (KJV). They remind us that the source of grace and peace is in God and Christ. In these simple words, *grace* and *peace,* is encompassed God's answer to all of man's need, for grace is that which provides the source of all spiritual blessings and particularly the blessing of salvation through Christ, and peace, that wholeness which grace brings. The joining of God and Jesus Christ with the single preposition "from" and the conjunction "and" place the Father and the Son as equals, and exhibits Paul's acceptance of the full deity of Christ.

Persecution seemed to be the peculiar lot of the church at Thessalonica. It was born in persecution (Acts 17:1–9) and grew in spite of continued tribulation (1 Thess. 1:6; 2:14; 3:1–3). Some of the believers, however, seemed to be asking the question, Why do we have to suffer? To do so was only natural, so in this chapter Paul gives them a prescription for persecution, and like all good prescriptions it was a combination of several ingredients.

2
ENCOURAGEMENT FROM PAUL'S GRATITUDE FOR THEIR GROWTH AND ENDURANCE

1:3–4

SECTION 1: ENCOURAGEMENT IN PERSECUTION, 1:3–12

THE OBLIGATION PAUL FELT TO BE THANKFUL, 1:3

Because of the steadfastness, or endurance, of the believers under trial and in spite of the problems and weakness in the group, Paul took every occasion to be thankful for them, and he does in verse 3. "We ought always to give thanks to God" appears stiff at first glance, but it indicates that some of the believers had apparently disclaimed the praise that Paul gave them in the first letter. So by using the words "we ought," he shows that the state of their spiritual condition compelled him to praise them. The thought is taken further in the phrase "as is only fitting," which indicates that the praise Paul was showering on them was no more than they deserved.

THE CONTENT OF PAUL'S THANKSGIVING, 1:3

What was it in the lives of the Thessalonians that called forth such commendation from the apostle? It included two things.

First of all, their faith continued to grow. Earlier, Paul had been anxious about the faith of his converts (1 Thess. 3:2, 5) and had written the former letter in order to help perfect, or complete, that which was lacking in their faith (1 Thess. 3:10). Now, a very short time later, he is able to give thanks for the fact that their faith had grown to a degree beyond his hopes. The verb "grows exceedingly" (NKJV) *(huperauxano)* is a very strong compound found only here in the New Testament and pictures growth as of a healthy plant.

Faith will always grow as one comes to know more about the One in whom his faith has been placed, and certainly one should come to know the Lord better in times of difficulties. This accounts, in part at least, for the growth of the Thessalonians' faith. Faith also grows as one sees the Lord working through him or her, and this too was true in their case, for theirs was a working faith (1 Thess. 1:3). Persecution helps faith to grow, and a growing faith is a bulwark in times of persecution.

Second, Paul gives thanks for their love (v. 3b). This too was an answer to his prayer (1 Thess. 3:12). Love is that which seeks the will of God in the one loved, and this the Thessalonians did in relation to all in the church. "Is greatly enlarged" has a different connotation from the verb "grows exceedingly" in the first part of the verse. It means "to overspread" as a fire or a flood covers everything in its path. Thus genuine Christian love shed abroad in our hearts by the Holy Spirit (Rom. 5:5) in obedience to the Lord's new commandment (John 13:34) will embrace every other member of the Christian group, not picking and choosing or rejecting this or that person. In this instance it overflowed all, even the disorderly idlers. So it should do today in all of our churches.

THE CONSEQUENCE OF PAUL'S THANKSGIVING, 1:4

Because of a growing faith and an expansive love, not only were the Thessalonians' hearts kept right in the midst of persecution, but also as a consequence ("therefore," v. 4), he was able to boast in all the churches of their constancy under trial. "Speak proudly" means "boast" and is an emphatic compound indicating that although it was not Paul's custom to do this, the case of the Thessalonians was so outstanding that even the founder of the church was compelled to sing her praises. It is of their patience and faith that he boasts.

"Perseverance" means a heroic, not weak, endurance under trial, and "faith" in this instance probably does not mean faithfulness (as is usually taken to be the meaning of *pistis* faith in Gal. 5:22) but their trust in the Lord, which enabled them to endure under trials. "Afflictions" has a broader meaning than "persecutions" and includes *any* trouble that a Christian might have. "Persecution" is generally limited to the attacks made on a believer because of his Christian stand. Both persecutions and afflictions continued to be the lot of the Thessalonians, for they were still enduring them when Paul wrote (the verb "endure" is in the present continuous tense).

3

ENCOURAGEMENT FROM THE KNOWLEDGE OF ULTIMATE RELIEF AND VINDICATION

1:5–10

Paul had apparently received a report that some of the believers were beginning to wonder if their difficulties did not deny rather than affirm the righteousness of God. If He is righteous, why do they have to suffer? This question he deals with in verses 5 through 10.

Difficulty in understanding the meaning of verse 5 is encountered only if the verse is made to refer to tribulations and persecutions as if they alone were a manifest token of the righteous judgment of God. However, the meaning of the verse is clear if the manifest token of the righteous judgment of God is the endurance and faith of the Thessalonians in the midst of persecutions (v. 4). Not suffering itself but their attitude of faith and constancy in suffering is the proof he cites.

In other words, since endurance could only be the working of God within the believer (and sometimes it is only in the times of trial that such working of God can be irrefutably demonstrated), this proves that God can declare the believer's worth to be a partaker of the kingdom. "Consider worthy" *(kataxioo)* means "to declare or count worthy," not "make worthy" (like *dikaioo*, "justify, or declare righteous"). Thus the Thessalonians are urged to view their endurance as a proof of God's working in them and a guarantee that He will keep His promises concerning their future place in the kingdom. When Christ returns, righteous and unrighteous will be separated, and the believers in Thessalonica are assured that they will be among the righteous.

From this specific deduction, Paul moves to certain general statements concerning the judgment of God. Verse 6 states the unassailable fact that God will bring judgment on the wicked and particularly upon those who were persecuting the Thessalonians. It is an illustration of the principle that whatever a man sows he will reap (Gal. 6:7), for God will pay back with affliction those who bring affliction on His people. Verse 7 exhorts the believers to relax in the knowledge that Christ's coming will be relief from and the righting of every wrong. "Rest" (v. 7 KJV) means "relief from tension" or "slackening of pressure," as when one takes down a taut bowstring (cf. Acts 24:23; 2 Cor. 2:13; 7:5; 8:13 for the only other uses in the New Testament). Paul is not saying that the Christian will be free from trouble until Christ comes, but he does assert that there can be rest in the midst of trial. And Paul includes himself among those who are being persecuted and who will enjoy this rest ("with us" KJV).

The coming of Christ will bring with it two things about which these believers needed instruction so that they would be garrisoned in persecution (7b–10). The first is retribution (7b–9). This happens not only *at* the time of His coming but it is included *in* it ("when . . ." is literally "in the revelation . . . ," v. 7b). The preposition "seems to be more than temporal, indicating the time of judgment; it also has instrumental implications, suggesting that the revelation is the means by which the requital is accomplished" (Hiebert, *The Thessalonian Epistles,* 288).

Christ's appearing will come with great power. He comes from heaven, accompanied by angels of His power (it is possible to translate as in the King James Version "mighty angels," but it is better to understand the genitive in the regular way, "angels of His power"), and in "flaming fire." The latter phrase continues to describe Christ's person and not His work. In other words, the flaming fire is the robe of the Lord in which He appears at His coming. It is an awesome description of His appearing at His second coming after the Tribulation (cf. Matt. 24:29–31). Vengeance on those who have not obeyed the Gospel by receiving the Savior is meted out at this coming, and it is in the form of everlasting destruction from the presence of the Lord (v. 9).

"Penalty" comes from the same root as the word *righteous.* Thus the punishment is not vindictive but deserved. The phrase "everlasting destruction" (KJV) occurs only here in the New Testament and is everything opposite from eternal life. It is not annihilation but separation from the presence (literally "face," *prosopon*) of God and the manifestation of His power. (Note, however, even throughout eternity, eternal punishment of the wicked will be in the sight, *enopion,* of the angels and of the Lord, Rev. 14:10). Throughout these verses, the power of God is pointedly emphasized to remind the Thessalonians that even though their present adversaries seem so powerful, there is One who is mightier than all, who will mete out punishment on their tormentors when He appears in great power and glory.

But the second coming of Christ will also be a time of glorification of Christ as well as a time of retribution. Two very amazing statements are contained in verse 10. First, when He comes He will be glorified *in* (not *by*) His saints (the word for the preposition "in" is prefixed to the verb for "to be glorified" as well as standing alone after the verb). In other words, Paul is making the astounding claim that the glory of the Lord will be mirrored in believers (cf. John 17:1; Eph. 2:7). Only the grace of God can lift a sinner to the place where he becomes the means of reflecting the glory of God.

Second, Christ at His coming will be admired or breathtakingly wondered at in those who believe. Again, Christians are stated to be the ones who bring admiration to the Lord on the part of those who witness His return. The spectators of His coming will marvel greatly at the Lord because they will then see fully displayed His grace in the completely changed lives of His people. The world today should see the same thing, albeit to a lesser degree, in the lives of Christians as they reflect the grace and glory of Christ. In verse 10, Paul seems to be saying that Christ will be admired in all that believe (and in the Thessalonians too, because his testimony was believed by them). The general statement "all who have believed" is specifically applied to the Thessalonians. The knowledge of that which Christ shall do at His coming, then, will effect a basic relaxation in the midst of the trials of this life.

4

ENCOURAGEMENT FROM KNOWING PAUL WAS PRAYING FOR THEM

1:11–12

Paul's prayer is addressed to "our God"—the God both Paul and the Thessalonians knew and served—asking that He may be able to count, or declare, the Thessalonians worthy (cf. comments on v. 5) of their high calling as Christians. This will be done only if, in turn, the believers fulfill all the good pleasure (or good resolve) of goodness (or every desire for goodness). Thus the reference is not to the goodness of God but to the goodness of the Thessalonians, and the clause may be translated "and fulfill all the good resolve of doing good." The fulfilling of the prayer depends on believers' having good resolve to do good in this world in spite of persecution. It is the principle of returning good for evil. Walking worthy, then, involves resolving to do good.

Coupled with this resolve is "the work of faith with power." As in 1 Thessalonians 1:3, faith is not viewed here as merely a passive thing but as an active use of the power of God in fruitful service. Thus Paul is praying that, even in the midst of persecution, the believers may be aggressive in performing good works and showing by their fruits that they serve the living and true God.

The result of such a life of good deeds and works of faith is that the name of Christ will be glorified (v. 12). One's name, of course, stands for the whole person, so that to glorify the name of the Lord is to show the world what the person of the Lord is like. The phrase "and you in Him" emphasizes that close union which all believers have because we are in Christ, and it is interesting to note that the doctrine of being "in Christ" is found in this early epistle of Paul's. The Lord first revealed it in John 14:20 as something that would begin with the Spirit's coming on the Day of Pentecost (cf. John 15:4–8; 17:1, 10, 21–26). In other letters, Paul uses "in Him" in relation to key doctrines such as election (Eph. 1:4), forgiveness (Eph.1:7), and sanctification (1 Cor. 1:2), as well as to glorification here.

As in the previous verse, all of this is ascribed to the grace of God. It is not within the power of man to glorify God by his good works; yet in His grace He condescends to use and empower man so that he may perform good works and glorify his heavenly Father. This is what Paul prays God will do through these believers so that they may walk worthy of their calling, particularly in times of trial.

ADDENDUM:
THE RAPTURE DEBATE AND THIS PASSAGE

Some (not all) posttribulationists (those who believe the rapture of the church will occur at the end of the Tribulation in connection with the Second Coming) understand verses 5–10 as supporting that position (see Gundry, *The Church and the Tribulation*, 113). Their argument goes like this: Since relief from persecution comes at the Second Coming, and that relief has to be associated with the Rapture, the Rapture must be at the same time as the Second Coming and not seven years before, as pretribulationists believe. Before embracing this posttribulational conclusion, however, observe and think about the following:

1. The Rapture is not specifically (even in a passing way) mentioned in these verses. Words such as "just" (v. 6), "repay" (v. 6), "flaming fire" (v. 7), and "retribution" (v. 8) do occur, but none of these words are used in connection with the Rapture (1 Cor. 15:51–58; 1 Thess. 4:13–18).
2. In this passage, Paul is emphasizing retribution on those who have persecuted believers. This will not happen until the Second Coming. It is the knowledge and assurance that persecutors will not go unpunished that Paul uses to sustain believers in all ages.
3. Relief from persecution for most believers has or will come at death. At the Rapture, only those living at that time will experience relief. Obviously the majority of believers will experience relief at death.
4. Granted, only persecutors living at the Second Coming will be judged then. Dead persecutors will be judged 1,000 years later at the resurrection related to the Great White Throne judgment. All premillennialists, regardless of their view of the time of the Rapture, would agree. But at the Second Coming there will be a vindication, though not the final one, of those who have suffered.
5. Notice the case of the martyrs of the Tribulation in Revelatio)–11. Because they are in heaven, they have obviously ven released from persecution through death. But

they cry out for vindication, which the Lord tells them will come later.

6. This passage does not teach that release from persecution will necessarily occur at the same time as the Second Coming (and posttribulation rapture). It does not describe the Rapture at all but focuses on judgment on those wicked living at the Second Coming and vindication of Christ's righteous judgment on them. That vindication gives assurance to saints of all ages that righteousness will prevail.

REVIEW QUESTIONS

1. What did Paul boast about the Thessalonians (1:4)?
2. How does enduring afflictions show that one can be counted worthy of the kingdom (1:4–5)?
3. When will Christ deal with those who persecute believers?
4. Is the rapture of the church specifically mentioned in this chapter?
5. How do posttribulationists attempt to support their view from this chapter?

5

THE DAY OF THE LORD
AND THE PRESENT

2:1–2

SECTION 2: ENCOURAGEMENT
FROM PROPHECY, 2:1–17

Paul did not hesitate to teach prophecy to *new* converts, for 1 and 2 Thessalonians are clear proof of this. Even during his short stay in Thessalonica, he had taught them many of the details of things to come (2 Thess. 2:5), and both epistles are filled with allusions to these matters. This example ought to encourage Christian workers not to avoid teaching prophecy even to new converts, and it counters a common argument that prophecy is too hard for people to understand. Paul obviously did not think so.

However, some had not fully or correctly comprehended all that Paul taught. The fact that some believers had died without entering the millennial kingdom became a problem, and Paul deals with this in 1 Thessalonians 4:13–18. In the following paragraph (5:1–11) he discusses the Day of the Lord, which from the Old Testament use of the term (to which he refers his readers) includes both the judgment of the Tribulation and the blessing of the Millennium. But it was not the millennial aspect of the Day of the Lord that confused the believers; rather, it was the judgments at the beginning of that Day about which they were unclear.

In 1 Thessalonians 5:1–11, Paul tries to make clear that Christians, not being appointed to wrath, will escape those judgments because they will be raptured before the Tribulation begins. Nevertheless, some Thessalonian believers thought that the Day of the Lord had already come and that they were living in it, because of the persecutions and trials through which they were passing. It is to this point, the *coming* or *beginning* of the Day of the Lord, that Paul speaks in the section. He assures these believers (and us) that the Day had not yet come and would not come until certain other events occur. Beyond any question, believers would not be subject to the judgments of that Day (for the meaning and uses of "the Day of the Lord" see the discussion at 1 Thess. 5:1).

THE SUBJECT MATTER OF PAUL'S TEACHING, 2:1

The subject as stated in the first verse is twofold—"the coming of our Lord Jesus Christ and our gathering together to Him." The word for "coming," *parousia,* means "presence" and is used by Paul in 1 Thessalonians 2:19 and 4:15 of the time when the church would be taken to be with Christ before the Tribulation begins. Sometimes the word is used of the return of Christ to the earth after the Tribulation (Matt. 24:37, 39).

Since the word used for "coming" means "presence," it could indicate that the Rapture and the Second Coming are a single event (posttribulationalism), or it could equally well indicate that His presence will be seen at the Rapture and also later at the Second Coming (pretribulationalism or midtribulationalism). The words for "our gathering together" are used elsewhere in the New Testament only in Hebrews 10:25 of the assembling of believers in a local church. In this passage it refers to the great gathering of living and dead believers in the air to meet their Lord and be with Him forever (1 Thess. 4:13–18). Thus the subject of the passage is clearly stated; it concerns the coming of Christ and in particular that aspect of it that involves our gathering together to meet Him.

THE PURPOSE OF PAUL'S TEACHING, 2:2

Word had circulated through the church that the Day of the Lord had already begun, which meant that the judgments of the beginning of that Day were already being experienced by the Thessalonians in the persecutions that they were then enduring.

These false reports had shaken some—the meaning of the word for "shake" pictures a restless tossing as of a ship, and the aorist tense indicates a kind of sudden shock—and they had created continual disturbance. The use of the present tense suggests a continuing state of agitation resulting from that shock.

The rumors that caused this disturbance had come in three ways. Some were saying that Paul had had a supernatural revelation that the Day of the Lord had already begun. This is the meaning of "by a spirit." The phrase refers to an alleged prophetic utterance some had pawned off on the congregation. (The phrase "as from us" is to be connected with "spirit," "word," and "letter" KJV.) Others either misrepresented or invented a message or report that Paul was teaching that the Day of the Lord was already present. Still others had evidently forged a letter as coming from Paul, in which it was declared that the Day of the Lord was present. Some make "letter" a reference to a misinterpretation of 1 Thessalonians, but in the light of what is written in 2 Thessalonians 3:17, it seems more likely that a spurious letter had been circulated. "As from us" is to be connected with "spirit," "message," and "letter."

THE BOTTOM LINE OF PAUL'S TEACHING, 2:2b

The truth Paul affirms is that the Day of the Lord is not yet present. The verb *enesteken* is used elsewhere in the New Testament to mean clearly "to be present" in contrast to something future (Rom. 8:38; 1 Cor. 3:22). Paul emphatically denies what some were erroneously teaching, namely, that some of the events of the many-sided Day of the Lord had already begun to take place.

6

THE DAY OF THE LORD,
THE APOSTASY, AND
THE LAWLESS ONE

2:3–5, 8–10

In order to prove his assertion that the Day of the Lord had not yet begun, Paul first cites the fact that the apostasy that must precede it had not yet appeared. Apostasy means a departure, and religious apostasy means departure from the truth. The definite article stands before the word "apostasy"; therefore, Paul is not talking about just any departure from the faith but about a special, particular, and widespread one. It is *the* apostasy that will come before the Day of the Lord. *Apostasia*, translated "apostasy," does not mean merely disbelieving but rather an aggressive and positive revolt (Acts 21:21; Heb. 3:12).

Paul himself later wrote in detail concerning the elements of this great departure from the faith, in 1 Timothy 4:1–3 and 2 Timothy 3:1–5; 4:3–4. In these passages he says that this defection would occur in the last days. It is as though the infidelity of those who profess to be religious will prepare the way and perhaps even furnish the base on which Antichrist will erect and promote his revolt against God and His truth. But the Day of the Lord will not come until this great religious apostasy sweeps the earth.

The Day of the Lord and the Lawless One

The Revelation of the Lawless One, 2:2–3b

Neither will the Day of the Lord begin until the Man of Sin, the "lawless one" (2:8), is revealed. This is the event that will begin that awful day of judgment. It is not his existence that is significant; it is his being revealed for what he is, that is, the Lawless One, which is the signal for the commencement of the events of that Day. Undoubtedly he will have been alive for some years before the Day begins, for he will have grown to manhood before instituting his terrible revolt against God. But he will be revealed when he makes a covenant with many of the Jewish people (Dan. 9:27), and this will signal the start of the Tribulation period. In this verse he is designated in two ways: the "man of lawlessness," which reveals his essential character as unalterably opposed to God and His law; and the "son of destruction," which assures his doom to eternal punishment as Judas, the other son of perdition, experienced (John 17:12; Acts 1:25). (The fact that Judas is called a son of perdition does not mean that the future man of lawlessness will be Judas resurrected.)

Elsewhere in the Bible this same personage is revealed as the "little horn" of Daniel 7:8, the "prince that shall come" of Daniel 9:26 (KJV), the "willful king" of Daniel 11:36, the "antichrist [who] shall come" of 1 John 2:18 (KJV), and the "beast coming up out of the sea" of Revelation 13:1–10. Although we are warned that there will appear from time to time evil men in the world—and so evil that they may be called antichrists (1 John 2:18)—this person is the ultimate personification of evil and the culmination of all that is opposed to God.

The Religion of the Lawless One, 2:4–5

In the Tribulation days, people will not be without religion. In the first half of the future Tribulation an ecumenical ecclesiastical organization or "church" will provide religion (Rev. 17). However, at the midpoint of the Tribulation, the Lawless One will overthrow that system (Rev. 17:16) and will seat himself in the temple in Jersualem and demand that people worship him. He opposes God (note the link with Satan in 1 Tim. 5:14, where the same participle is used but translated there "the enemy"). He will exalt himself above "every so-called god." The connotation is very broad—any so-called god as well as any object of worship. In other words, the Lawless One will endeavor to take first place over the true God, any and all false gods, and anything else that man worships. Furthermore, his religious system will be connected with the Jewish temple in Jerusalem. This is the abomination of desolation spoken of by Daniel 9:27 and attested to by our Lord (Matt. 24:15), which will stand in the holy place and require people to worship him.

All of this Paul had taught the Thessalonians when he was in their midst. The word for "told" in verse 5 (KJV) is in the imperfect tense, which indicates that he repeatedly told them of these matters relative to the Second Coming. This ought to be an encouragement to any who feel timid about teaching prophecy to new converts.

THE POWER OF THE LAWLESS ONE, 2:9–10

In verses 9 and 10 there are a number of descriptive words that vividly portray the power of the Antichrist. In general, his power and activity may be described as counterfeiting. He too will have a *parousia*, a coming, as will the Lord (v. 9). He also will be empowered, perhaps analogous to the Lord's being filled with the Spirit during His earthly ministry (Luke 4:1), except that the Antichrist's power will come from Satan (cf. Rev. 13:4). He will perform counterfeit miracles. They will be "in power" (cf. Luke 4:36); they will have meaning, for they are called "signs" (cf. John 2:11); and they will have the effect on people of being "wonders" (cf. John 4:48; Acts 2:22), i.e., things that cannot be explained. These will promote evil deception on those who are perishing, simply because they would not receive the truth and be saved. How widespread and how powerful will be this evil man's might to counterfeit the truth that is in Christ and His Gospel.

THE PUNISHMENT OF THE LAWLESS ONE, 2:8

Underlying this entire section, which so vividly describes the power of the Lawless One, is the firm note of the sovereign and almighty power of God. This is clearly seen in verse 8, where Paul describes the destruction of the Lawless One. His doom has already been mentioned as destruction (v. 3). Here the means of bringing it to pass is described as by "the breath of His mouth." This expression occurs only here in the New Testament and indicates a "sweeping away like a hurricane, or killing like the blast from a furnace" (Plummer, *A Commentary on St. Paul's Second Epistle to the Thessalonians*, 64).

Parallel to this idea is the expression in the last part of the verse: "the appearance of His coming." The very appearance of the Lord will effect the end of the Lawless One's program though not of his existence. The "end" of the Antichrist is not annihilation. It is a putting out of business, for the verb translated "destroy" actually means "to make idle" or "render inoperative" (cf. Rom. 6:6). The earthly activities of the Antichrist will be terminated by being cast alive into the lake of fire (Rev. 19:20), and he will remain alive in that place for all eternity (cf. Rev. 20:10). This is his certain punishment, and it is as sure as the power of God.

7

THE DAY OF THE LORD AND THE RESTRAINER

2:6–7

Verse 8 begins with a word that indicates sequence of events—*tote,* "then." It stands in sharp contrast to "now" in verse 6 and "already" and "now" in verse 7. When the restrainer is taken out of the way, *then* the Lawless One will be revealed. We have already been told that the Day of the Lord cannot begin until the Lawless One is revealed, and he cannot be revealed until the restrainer is removed, so it follows that the Day of the Lord cannot begin, either, until the restrainer is removed. Paul distinguishes this order of events very clearly.

Not only is the order of events apparent, but so is the work of the restrainer. It is described by the word "restrains." This word can mean "hold fast" (as in 1 Thess. 5:21) or "hold back" (as here and Rom. 1:18). The restrainer holds back the full manifestation of evil in the person of the Lawless One, and that is why he cannot be revealed until the restrainer is removed. That evil is already at work is affirmed in verse 7, but its fullest revelation will come with the appearance of the Lawless One.

The fact of restraining is clear from these verses, but who and/or what does it is the matter that is debated. In verse 6, "what restrains" is a neuter participle with the neuter article. In verse 7, "he who now restrains" is a masculine participle with the masculine article. Furthermore, Paul says that the Thessalonians were acquainted with what it is that restrains (v. 6). Also, in order to restrain the Lawless One, who will be empowered by Satan, the restrainer must be more powerful than Satan in order to hold back this evil person. Thus the facts in the text tell us (1) that the restrainer is a principle, (2) that the restrainer is a person, (3) that the identification was well known to the readers, and (4) that the power of the restrainer must be greater than Satan's.

Most commentators identify the restrainer with the Roman Empire of Paul's day, which held back evil by its advanced system of laws, many of which are still basic to legal systems of our day. It is admitted, however, by those who hold this view that the restrainer is not merely the Roman Empire but government in general, since it is only too apparent that the Lawless One did not make his appearance at the end of the Roman Empire. Support for this view is cited from Paul's own statement that governments are ordained of God for the purpose of restraining evil (Rom. 13:1–7). However, it must be recognized that governments do not always fulfill their ordained purpose, and, furthermore, no government nor all governments put together can be stronger in power than Satan. It should also be remembered that the Tribulation period, during which the Lawless One holds sway, will be a time of superstrong, dictatorial government.

Other suggestions for the identity of the restrainer include Satan (but v. 7 precludes this interpretation), some powerful angel (but Jude 9, which shows the impotence of the archangel in the face of satanic opposition, argues against this), or no positive identification at all. It is sometimes asserted that Paul himself was unsure (but how did the Thessalonians know, if Paul did not teach them, vv. 5–6?), or, more often, that even though Paul and his readers knew, we who read this letter today cannot know.

Ultimately a decision as to the identity of the restrainer will be made on the basis of answering the question, Who is powerful enough to hold back Satan? The obvious and only answer to that question is God. Therefore, the restrainer must be God Himself. In this view, the neuter used in verse 6 would remind us of the power of God in general, and the masculine in verse 7 would point to the person of God. Most premillennialists further identify the restrainer as the third person of the Godhead, the Holy Spirit. The fact that one of the first specific mentions of the work of the Holy Spirit is that of His restraining (Gen. 6:3) adds support to this interpretation.

Regarding the use of both the neuter and masculine, it may be suggested that the use of the neuter in verse 6 is to be accounted for by the fact that the Greek word for *Spirit* is itself neuter. The masculine in verse 7 would indicate that the Spirit is a person who should be referred to in the masculine gender (as is done in John 15:26; 16:13–14; Eph. 1:13–14).

"To one familiar with the Lord Jesus' Upper Room Discourse, as Paul undoubtedly was, fluctuation between neuter and masculine recalls how the Holy Spirit is spoken of. Either gender is appropriate, depending on whether the speaker (or writer) thinks of natural agreement (masculine because of the Spirit's personality) or grammatical (neuter because of the noun *pneuma*: John 14:26; 15:26; 16:13)" (Thomas, "Second Thessalonians," in *The Expositor's Bible*, 11:324).

It is really impossible to see how the restrainer can be anyone other than God Himself. Undoubtedly, God uses good government, elect angels, and other means to restrain evil, but the ultimate power behind such forceful restraint must be the power of God and the person of God. This much appears to be beyond question. Whether Paul is specifically referring to the Holy Spirit in this passage may be debatable—though it is recognized that restraining is elsewhere said to be His work (Gen. 6:3; John 16:7–11; 1 John 4:4). However, it should be clearly recognized that whether or not this further identification of the restrainer as the Spirit is made does not affect the argument for a pretribulation rapture of the church.

That pretribulation argument is simply this: The restrainer is God, and the instrument of restraint is the God-indwelt church (cf. Eph. 4:6 for God indwelling; Gal. 2:20 for Christ indwelling; 1 Cor. 6:19 for the Spirit indwelling). It should be remembered Christ said of the divinely indwelt and empowered church that "the gates of hell shall not prevail against it" (Matt. 16:18 KJV), so we can say that this indwelt, empowered church is an adequate restraining instrument against the forces of darkness. The church will not go through any of the Tribulation because the restrainer will be removed before the Lawless One is revealed, which revelation by signing the covenant with the Jews (Dan. 9:27) begins the Tribulation period. Since the restrainer is ultimately God, and since God indwells all Christians, either He must be withdrawn from the hearts of believers while they are left on earth to go through the Tribulation, or else, when He is withdrawn, all believers are taken with Him. Since it is impossible for a believer to be "disindwelt," the only alternative is that believers too will be taken out of the way before the appearance of the Lawless One, which signals the start of the Tribulation.

Against this interpretation it is usually argued that "it is difficult to see in what sense either [the Father or the Spirit] could *be taken out of the way* (verse 7)" (Morris, *The Epistles of Paul to the Thessalonians*, 130). The answer to this is to differentiate between *residence* and *presence*. Every person of the Godhead has been, is, and always will be present in the world simply because God is omnipresent. But the persons of the Godhead, and particularly the Holy Spirit, have not always been resident within the hearts of God's people either permanently or universally (see John 14:17, where the preposition *with* describes the relationship of the Holy Spirit in the Old Testament, whereas the preposition *in* describes it in the New Testament). Today God has guaranteed to be always resident within the hearts of all of His people (cf. Rom. 8:9; 1 Cor. 6:19).

Thus, to say that the restrainer is removed is not to say that the presence of God is taken away from the earth, nor is it to imply that God (specifically the Holy Spirit) will cease to work in the world. Many will be saved in the Tribulation period (cf. Rev. 7:14), and God will be the One who accomplishes that work just as He did in Old Testament times and as He does now. God's universal and permanent residence in His people is a distinctive relationship in this day of grace, and certainly the removal of His residence (including those believers in whom He resides) does not mean the withdrawal of His presence or the cessation of His activity. This interpretation does full justice to all the facts and implications of this passage.

8

THE DAY OF THE LORD
AND UNBELIEVERS

2:10–12

In the middle of verse 10 the spotlight is put on those who follow the Lawless One and believe his lie. Because they receive
not the truth, they perish (the participle is in the present tense,
indicating that they are already perishing, even though they are
yet alive). Verses 11 and 12 set forth the consequence of this
unbelief, the opening phrase, "For this reason," pointing back
to verse 10. It is that God sends strong delusion. The two words
translated "strong delusion" (KJV) mean literally "a powerful
working of error," and the sending of it is attributed to God. It
might seem that this sending of delusion ought to be the work
of Satan, but it is the sovereign God who inflicts it on man
because he did not receive the truth when he had the chance.

One purpose of the delusion is that men may believe "the"
(NIV) lie of Satan as proclaimed by the Lawless One (not "a lie,"
as in the King James Version, because the definite article is in the
original text). All men are believers in something, and in these
future days they will either believe the truth of God or believe
the lie of Satan. A second purpose of God's sending the strong
delusion is stated in verse 12—that all such unbelievers may be
condemned. The justification for their judgment is simply that

they believed not the truth and rejoiced in iniquity. It is a picture of lowest degradation and complete opposition to God and His truth. The Lawless One may have widespread success for a time, but it is God who will ultimately triumph over all evil.

A question often arises from these verses and a general knowledge of the Tribulation as to whether people who have heard the Gospel in this period before the Rapture will have another opportunity to believe and be saved after the Tribulation begins. We do know for certain that multitudes of people will be saved during the Tribulation (the 144,000 and the great multitude which cannot be numbered, Rev. 7:4 and 9). We also know that multitudes will rebel against Christ and follow Antichrist (Rev. 9:20–21; 13:14; 16:14).

But back to the original question. These verses indicate that those who did not receive the love of the truth (v. 10), who believed what was false (literally, the lie [of Antichrist], v. 11), who did not believe the truth (v. 12), and who had pleasure in wickedness (v. 12) will perish (v. 10) and be judged (v. 12). All these phrases point to the conclusion that rejecters in this age will not become acceptors in the Tribulation. Logic might dictate otherwise, for how could people who have been exposed to the truth in this time fail to understand what is happening when the Tribulation begins, and turn from their unbelief to faith? But we must factor into the equation the hardness of people's hearts and the "deluding influence" God will send (v. 11).

But the question that is difficult or close to impossible to answer is this: How much rejection will condemn a person? The tenses of the verbs in verses 10 and 12 indicate a deliberate and sustained rejection, not a casual one. Is listening to a Gospel message in church or on the radio or TV and not receiving the message sufficient rejection? I would like to think not. Indifference now (even though it involves hearing the Gospel) may not rule out an acceptance of the Gospel in the Tribulation. But hardness brought on by continued rejection seems more likely to carry over into the Tribulation and become even more rigid, so as to rule out any acceptance of the truth. This is a difficult question to answer clearly, and although one hopes everybody (including present rejecters) will have opportunity and will accept the Savior during the Tribulation, one must consider the import of these verses.

9

THE DAY OF THE LORD AND BELIEVERS

2:13–17

In this last paragraph of the chapter, Paul turns from the awful contemplation of Antichrist and the doom of his followers to the bright prospect that belongs to the Thessalonians and all other believers everywhere. Again as in 1:3, his thoughts are cast in the form of a thanksgiving made necessary because of what God had done in their hearts.

THE BELIEVER'S POSITION, 2:13–14

Two things are said about a believer's position, which are the basis for his prospect. He has been chosen (v. 13) and called (v. 14). The word Paul uses to describe the choosing is an unusual one and is used nowhere else in the New Testament of divine election (though it is used otherwise in Phil. 1:22 and Heb. 11:25). In the Greek Old Testament it is used in relation to God's choosing Israel (Deut. 26:18). The time when this choosing was done is said to be the "beginning." Some understand this to mean the beginning of the preaching mission in Thessalonica, but it is better to see "from the beginning" as a reference to the beginning of all things, i.e., from before the world began.

That election was before time began is an idea that is regularly found in Paul's writings (1 Cor. 2:7; Eph. 1:4). God had the choice of His people in mind in eternity past. The end purpose of the choosing was salvation, and this was accomplished "through sanctification of the Spirit and belief of the truth" (KJV). In this phrase, the divine and human responsibilities in salvation are placed together. On God's part, being saved involves the work of the Holy Spirit in sanctifying, or setting apart, the believer. This refers to that sanctification of position as belonging to God that every Christian has the moment he believes (1 Cor. 6:11). The human responsibility is to believe the truth, and the two aspects are linked inseparably, as shown by the single occurrence of the preposition "in."

While the "choosing" of verse 13 was in eternity, the "calling" of verse 14 is related to time. It was accomplished through the preaching of the Gospel and involves the obtaining of glory in a future day (cf. 1:10). There is a great deal of deep theology bound up in the simple statements of these two verses, and, like all theology, it had its practical use—in this case encouraging the Thessalonians in their difficulties and trials.

The Believer's Practice, 2:15–17

Therefore, since believers were included in the pre-temporal purpose of God and are guaranteed ultimately the glory of God, and since believers cannot be overcome by Satan or his Lawless One, therefore stand fast in the midst of opposition from the enemies of Christ and in the face of uncertainty of the time of the return of Christ.

Furthermore, believers are exhorted to hold fast the "traditions" of Christ. The word *traditions* does not mean things that people have made up but things that have been passed on from one to another and which were received in the first place from God Himself. "The prominent idea of *paradosis* [tradition] then in the New Testament is that of an authority external to the teacher himself" (Lightfoot, *Notes on Epistles of St Paul from unpublished commentaries,* 21). These teachings from God were handed on by word and by letter (1 Cor. 11:2; 2 Thess.

3:6; cf. Rom. 6:17; 1 Cor. 15:3; 2 Tim. 1:13), and, whether by letter or word, they were authoritative.

The section closes with prayer for strength to stand fast and hold fast the traditions. It invokes the help of Christ and the Father, who loves us (as exhibited at Calvary) and who has given "everlasting comfort" (KJV) or encouragement (which word includes the idea of strength) and "good hope" based on the grace of God. The help comes in the form of comfort and strengthening (v. 17). Strength and stability in every good word and work is Paul's prayer for his beloved believers. "It is the rousing and cheering of the whole inner man which the Apostles pray for—that the Thessalonians may be animated to brave endurance and vigorous activity" (Findlay, *The Epistles of Paul the Apostle to the Thessalonians,* 194).

To sum up this chapter, Paul's message is: Do not be disturbed, for the Day of the Lord has not yet come. When it does come, it will be a terrible time of revealing the power of Satan through his Antichrist, the Lawless One. But you believers will not experience these awful things, for your prospect is glory, not wrath. In the meantime, however, maintain a strong and stable Christian testimony in every word and work.

SOME REVIEW QUESTIONS

1. What part of the Day of the Lord does Paul emphasize in 2:2?
2. What does apostasy mean?
3. What are some other names for the Lawless One in the Bible?
4. Give some details about the Lawless One's religion.
5. Give some views as to the identify of the restrainer. Which do you prefer?
6. Why is it important to distinguish between the residence and the presence of the Holy Spirit?

10
PAUL'S REQUEST
FOR CONTINUED PRAYER

3:1–2

SECTION 3: ENCOURAGEMENT AND COMMANDS
CONCERNING VARIOUS PRACTICES, 3:1–18

The first word of chapter 3, "finally," indicates the end of the principal doctrinal discussions of the letter and the beginning of the conclusion (as 1 Thess. 4:1).

Paul's request for prayer is in the present tense in verse 1 and evidently means that Paul had heard that the Thessalonians were praying for him. He encourages them to keep on doing it. His petitions are twofold. First, he asks them to continue praying that the word of the Lord may spread rapidly and be glorified. "May spread rapidly" (NIV) translates the single word meaning "run." Both "run" and "be glorified" are in the present tense, signifying that the request is for a continuously swift advance and success of the word of the Lord. Paul uses "Lord," referring to Jesus Christ, twenty-two times in these two letters (Milligan, *St Paul's Epistles to the Thessalonians*, 137). The second petition, for deliverance (v. 2), relates to the first. The success of the Gospel and safety for its messengers are interrelated.

Although we can appreciate Paul's natural desire for self-protection, his greater motive for this request is the advancement of the Gospel. The definite article (not translated) before "perverse and evil men" points to a particular deliverance from specific enemies who were giving him trouble at that time. The reference must be to the Jews who were troubling him, i.e., to the Jews who opposed the apostle's ministry in Corinth (Acts 18:1–18). The last phrase in the verse, "for not all have faith," reminds his readers that opposition is to be expected, simply because not all are believers and either do not share or are directly opposed to what Christianity stands for.

11

PAUL'S CONFIDENCE
AND HIS PRAYER

3:3–5

Verses 3 and 4 give a word of encouragement concerning the faithfulness of Christ in contrast to the lack of faith in those referred to in verse 2. Not all have faith, but faithful is the Lord who "will strengthen and protect you." We might have expected Paul to say "us," but his converts take top priority. He also assures them that God's faithfulness will keep them from "evil."

The form of the word "evil" can be either masculine (the evil one, Satan) or neuter (evil things). Probably we are to understand it here as a reference to Satan, in light of Paul's previous concern relative to Satan's attacks as expressed in 1 Thessalonians 3:5. Or perhaps both ideas are included (cf. Matt. 6:13). His confidence in the faithfulness of God also extends to their keeping his commandments, both those he had given them and those that he was about to give them in verses 6 through 15. It is a tactful way to introduce what follows (v. 4).

PAUL'S PRAYER, 3:5

This expression of confidence in God leads Paul to breathe a short prayer, which concludes these introductory verses to the chapter. It is one of those very few prayers in the New Testament addressed to the Lord Jesus (for another, see Acts 7:60), and it concerns two things about the inner lives of the Thessalonian believers.

First, he prays that their hearts may be directed into the love of God. If the genitive "of God" is subjective, it means our love for God; and if it is objective, it means His love for us. Possibly both ideas are included here; thus Paul prays that the believers may realize fully what God's love for them means and in return love Him more.

Second, he prays that their hearts may be directed into the "steadfastness" (not passive patient waiting, but positive and active endurance as in 1 Thess. 1:3) of Christ. In other words, he is asking that they might reproduce the endurance in the face of trials that Christ exhibited in His own life on earth. Paul's other prayers for the Thessalonians in this letter are recorded in 1:11–12 and 2:16–17.

12

THE UNRULY
AND BUSYBODIES

3:6–12

This fairly lengthy section shows how aggravated the problem of laziness had become in the church since the writing of 1 Thessalonians (cf. 4:11–12; 5:14). Doctrinal misconception had resulted in practical misconduct, as it often does. Misunderstanding the truths involved in Christ's second coming had led some to expect that they would not have to work anymore until the Lord came. Paul's admonitions in the first letter had not nipped the problem in the bud; thus this extremely authoritative section.

THE PENALTY FOR THE UNRULY, 3:6

The erring brethren are designated as those who walk disorderly, or in an "unruly" manner. This is a military term and means "those out of rank." Concerning such, Paul gives a command "in the name of our Lord Jesus Christ." This expression is as authoritative as Paul can make it, and yet at the same time he recognizes the unruly person as a "brother." The command is to withdraw, or keep aloof from, the brother who is out of rank. The word for "aloof, away from" is used elsewhere in the New Testament in 2 Corinthians 8:20 only. It pictures the furling of sails or the gathering together of a robe as a sign of disgust. This is not a withdrawal with an air of superiority, but it is an aloofness that signifies no condoning of the deeds of the disorderly. This penalty is more stern than what Paul wrote in 1 Thessalonians 5:14, and while it did not mean excommunication from the group, it likely did mean that these unruly people were not to be allowed to participate in the Lord's Supper.

The Pattern for the Unruly: Paul's Own Conduct, 3:7–9

The unruliness in these verses is not general but refers specifically to the refusal of these people to earn their own living and their sponging off other believers. Paul reminds his readers again (cf. 1 Thess. 1:5; 2:9) of his own example of working to support himself and exhorts them to follow (literally, "imitate") him in this regard. Indeed it is more than an exhortation that is stated in verse 7—it is an obligation that is imposed ("you ought"). Paul's example was of hard work (v. 8), which included nighttime work in order that he would not have to be dependent on anyone else for his support. It is also an example of humble willingness (v. 9), for he reminds them that although he had the right to receive financial support from them, he waived that right in order to set a good example (literally, "a type") for them.

The Prescription for Unruliness, 3:10

The clear-cut rule that Paul laid down when he was with them was this: "If any would not work, neither should he eat" (KJV). This may have been a common saying of the day, which Paul simply took over and gave his sanction to. Simply stated, the prescription is: no work, no eat.

Commands Concerning Busybodies, 3:11–12

Particular cases had evidently been reported to Paul anonymously, which he now deals with in these verses. These people were misusing their time. They were busybodies instead of being busy. There is a neat play on the Greek words in verse 11, since the word *busybody* is built on the root of the word *work*. The adjectival form for "busybody" is found in 1 Timothy 5:13. Probably these brethren were busily trying to convert others to the idea that they too should quit working in view of the nearness of the Lord's return. Instead, they should have been working so that they could support themselves (v. 12). This should be accompanied by an inner peace and tranquility to replace the state of agitation they were in over the Second Coming.

13
FURTHER ENCOURAGEMENT
AND COMMANDS

3:13–15

Finally, to all Paul says "do not grow weary of doing good" (v. 13). "Do not grow weary" means "do not lose heart"—an inner discouragement, not physical weariness (cf. Luke 18:1; 2 Cor. 4:1, 16; Gal. 6:9 for the only other occurrences of this expression)—and "doing good" means "doing the noble thing." However long the Lord may delay His coming, and whatever disorderliness others may engage in, we should constantly conduct ourselves according to the highest standards of work, discipline, orderliness, quietness, and doing good, and exhibit these traits without faltering.

CONCERNING THE DISOBEDIENT, 3:14–15

Paul, remembering how his former admonition had been neglected, now directs the church as to what to do in case the more obstinate offenders disregard his present commands. His advice is threefold.

First, the disobedient one is to be noted (v. 14). "Note" has the connotation of marking something or branding. In other words, the church is to mark off with disapproval anyone who does not obey what Paul writes in this letter. Though the command to brand such a one is clear, the means of doing so are not stated. Perhaps it involved some sort of congregational censure.

Second, the believers are not to "associate with" anyone who disobeys these commands (v. 14). This verb literally means "don't mix yourselves up with him." It prohibits familiar fellowship in order that, being cut off from the company of fellow believers, the disobedient one may be ashamed. The object of this isolation of the erring brother is remedial, not vindictive.

Third, the sinning brother is to be admonished (v. 15). The verb means "to put in mind of the truth." The purpose of this treatment of the disobedient one is to restore him to fellowship, and that is why Paul insists that the church remember that the person they are dealing with is a brother in the Lord. Perhaps he fears that some will be overzealous and take too drastic action, and it goes without saying that, when the offender confesses his wrong, he is to be forgiven and restored.

14

CONCLUSION

3:16–18

PAUL'S PRAYER FOR PEACE, 3:16

The epistle concludes with a prayer (v. 16), a salutation (v. 17), and a benediction (v. 18). The prayer is for tranquility of heart, and it has evidently come to Paul's mind because of the things he has just been discussing. It is only the "Lord of peace" who can give peace in the midst of trials and restlessness concerning the Second Coming. This peace for which Paul prays is one that will remain continually ("always"), that will not vary in spite of altering circumstances ("in every circumstance"), and that can be experienced because of the presence of the Lord with us ("the Lord be with you all").

PAUL'S PERSONAL GREETING, 3:17

The salutation of verse 17 is written by Paul's own hand, for, as was his custom, he dictated the letter to a secretary who wrote it down. But at the conclusion he himself takes the pen and adds a few words in his own handwriting (cf. Gal. 6:11). This was a sign of genuineness and was particularly needed in this letter because of the forged letter that had been circulated in his name (2:2).

PAUL'S PRAYER FOR GRACE, 3:18

The letter concludes with a customary benediction and one that was especially gracious in this instance, for it encompassed all the believers, even the ones whom Paul had to sharply rebuke in this letter. The great apostle's heart always went out to all his flock.

SOME REVIEW QUESTIONS

1. Are prayers normally addressed to Jesus (3:5 and Eph. 2:18)?
2. What were the unruly believers doing (or perhaps we should ask what they were not doing!) at Thessalonica?
3. What does it mean to "keep away from" (v. 6) these believers?
4. What three actions does Paul say to take against obstinate offenders (3:14–15)?

SELECTED BIBLIOGRAPHY

Deissmann, Adolf. *New Light on the New Testament*. Edinburgh: T. & T. Clark, 1907.

Donfield, Karl P. "The Cults of Thessalonica and the Thessalonian Correspondence," *New Testament Studies*. 31 (1985): 336–56.

Edgar, Thomas R. "The Meaning of 'Sleep' in 1 Thessalonians 5:10." *Journal of the Evangelical Society*, December 1979.

English, E. Schuyler. *Re-Thinking the Rapture*. Traveler's Rest, S.C.: Southern Bible Book House, 1954.

Findlay, G. G. *The Epistles of Paul the Apostle to the Thessalonians*. Cambridge Greek Testament. Cambridge: University Press, 1911.

Gundry, Robert N. *The Church and the Tribulation*. Grand Rapids: Zondervan, 1973.

Hiebert, D. Edmond. *The Thessalonian Epistles*. Chicago: Moody, 1971.

Hogg, C. F., and Vine, W. E. *The Epistles of Paul the Apostle to the Thessalonians.* Glasgow: Pickering & Inglis, n. d.

Lightfoot, J. B. *Notes on epistles of St Paul from unpublished commentaries.* London: Macmillan, 1895.

Milligan, George. *St Paul's Epistles to the Thessalonians.* Grand Rapids: Eerdmans, 1952.

Morris, Leon. *The Epistles of Paul to the Thessalonians.* Grand Rapids: Eerdmans, 1957.

Plummer, Alfred. *A Commentary on St. Paul's First Epistle to the Thessalonians.* London: Robert Scott, 1918.

_____. *A Commentary on St. Paul's Second Epistle to the Thessalonians.* London: Robert Scott, 1918.

Ramsay, W. M. *St. Paul the Traveller and the Roman Citizen.* London: Hodder and Stoughton, 1895.

Robinson, J. Armitage. *St. Paul's Epistle to the Ephesians.* London: Macmillan, 1914.

Salmon, George. *A Historical Introduction to the Study of the Books of the New Testament.* London: John Murray, 1892.

Sauer, Erich. *The Triumph of the Crucified.* Grand Rapids: Eerdmans, 1952.

Stacey, W. David. *The Pauline View of Man.* London: Macmillan, 1956.

Thomas, Robert L. "Second Thessalonians." The Expositor's Bible. Edited by Frank E. Gaebelein. Grand Rapids: Zondervan, 1978.

Walvoord, John F. *The Rapture Question.* Findlay, Ohio: Dunham, 1957.